Java For Newbies

The Ultimate Crash Course

Java For Newbies

The Ultimate Crash Course

By Doug Purcell

Contents

Intro..17

Chapter 1: The fast guide to running your first java program **19**

Under the hood 19

The components 20

Setting the system path 21

Writing your first java program 24

99 problems but my first program ain't one!......................................26

    Compiler errors 26

    Syntax errors...27

    Semantic errors 27

    Runtime errors 28

Chapter 1 Re-factored...28

Chapter 1 Resources 29

Chapter 1 Exercises...29

Chapter 1 Answers 31

Chapter 2: The insider guide to java primitive types.................................**32**

Integrals 32

byte 33

short 33

int 33

long 34

char 34

Floating point types 35

float 35

double 35

Booleans 36

Painless guide to binary, octals, and hexadecimals 36

Binary numbers 37

Octals 39

Hexadecimals 39

Literals 41

Integer literals 41

Floating point literals 41

Boolean literals 42

Char literals 42

Operators 42

Unary Operators Crash Course 43

Binary Operators Crash Course 45

Assignment, Equality, Relational, and Conditional 47

Bitwise Operators and Bit Shifts 51

Operator Precedence and Associativity 53

Widening and Narrowing Conversions 54

Widening primitive Conversions 54

Narrowing primitive Conversions 56

Variables in Java..57

    The rules...57

    The Conventions 58

    Comments...59

Chapter 2 Re-factored...60

Chapter 2 Resources 60

Chapter 2 Exercises 61

Chapter 2 Answers 62

Chapter 3: Making a statement **64**

Expressions, statements, and blocks 64

if-then statement 65

if-then-else statement 67

else-if 69

switch statement 71

    Rules for the switch statement...72

Looptopia 74

    do while 74

    while loop..75

    for loop..76

Nested loops...77

break...81

continue 82

Chapter 3 Re-factored 82

Chapter 3 Exercises..83

Chapter 3 Solutions...95

Chapter 4: Classes, Objects, and Methods, Oh My...........**108**

The real scoop about classes in java 108

Types of variables 109

packages...111

Importing classes 112

Access modifiers 113

Chart of access modifiers 114

Objects...114

      Creating objects 114

Methods..115

      A method that returns...116

      A method that's void 116

      Calling a method 117

      Overloading methods...119

Constructors 119

      Default values 123

      Overloading constructors...126

This keyword..126

Setters..127

Getters 128

Why use setters and getters? 129

Static fields 130

enums...131

      Creating enums 131

      Iterating over enums...132

      enums with switch statements...................................133

Chapter 4 Re-factored 136

Chapter 4 Exercises...137

Chapter 4 Exercises Answers...141

Chapter 5: Inheritance, Polymorphism, and Interfaces 146

Inheritance 146

The rules of inheritance...147

An example of inheritance 148

Method overriding 150

@Override annotation 151

Super keyword 152

This keyword..153

Polymorphism 155

Interfaces 160

How to declare an interface 160

The rules of interfaces..161

Why the heck would you use interfaces? 163

Blow-by-blow analysis..164

Extending interfaces 165

Default methods..165

Extending interfaces that contain default methods.............166

Static methods in interfaces...167

Interface example..167

Abstract classes 172

How are abstract classes different than regular classes? 172

How are abstract classes different than interfaces? 174

When to use an abstract class over an interface?.................176

Abstract class example..176

Nested classes...181

The benefits of nested classes 182

Static nested classes 182

Accessing members from static nested classes 183

Inner classes 184

    Accessing members from inner classes..184

Local classes 185

Anonymous classes 187

    The syntax for creating anonymous classes 187

    When to use anonymous classes..189

Class diagrams 189

    Class diagram through example 189

Chapter 5 Re-factored 200

Chapter 5 Resources 201

Chapter 5 Exercises..201

Chapter 5 Exercise Answers...202

Chapter 6: Strings..**203**

How to declare Strings 203

How to compare Strings 205

Concatenation 205

    Multiple line spans..206

    Printing mixed types 206

    Escape characters 208

Analyzing the String class in java 209

Chapter 6 Re-factored 214

Chapter 6 Resources 214

Chapter 6 Exercises..214

Chapter 6 Answers 215

Chapter 7 Arrays **217**

    The law of arrays...217

    Indexes and elements..218

    Boundaries 219

    Alternative array formats 219

    Iterating over arrays 220

    Manipulating elements in an array 221

    Passing arrays to constructors 222

    Passing arrays to methods 223

    Passing an array to the main method 224

    Copying arrays 224

    Multidimensional arrays 225

    A tour of the array class 226

    Chapter 7 Re-factored 229

    Chapter 7 Resources 229

    Chapter 7 Exercises..229

    Chapter 7 Answers 230

Chapter 8: Collections and Generics **232**

    The Collection Interface..232

    List Interface 234

    ArrayList..234

    How to create an ArrayList 235

        Intro to Generics 235

    A Demo of an ArrayList 237

    The classic for loop..238

    Iterator 239

    Enhanced for Loop 240

When to use an ArrayList 240

Wrapper Classes 241

LinkedList...243

    How to create a LinkedList 243

    A Demo of a LinkedList...244

    When to use a LinkedList 245

Stack..245

    A Demo of the Stack Class 246

    When to use a Stack 248

Queues...249

Sets 250

Maps...251

Chapter 8 Re-factored 252

Chapter 8 Resources 252

Chapter 8 Questions 253

Chapter 8 Answers..253

Chapter 9: Lambdas **255**

The benefits of lambdas in java..255

Functional interfaces..256

The syntax behind a lambda 258

@FunctionalInterface...260

Recap of lambda expression elements 260

java.util.function package 261

Method reference 264

Chapter 9 Re-factored 264

Chapter 9 Resources 265

Chapter 9 Questions 265

Chapter 9 Answers 267

Chapter 10: Java Classes **270**

Mathematics 270

    A Tour of the Math Class 270

    A Tour of BigDecimal..272

Random 275

The Scanner Class...276

    How to read data from a file into the Scanner object............................279

    Introduction to Exceptions 279

Intro to Java FX..281

    Integrating JavaFX with an IDE..281

    Eclipse 281

    Main.java Blow-by-blow Analysis 285

    Modifying Main.java 288

    Drawing shapes 289

    Creating buttons...293

Chapter 10 Re-factored 294

Chapter 10 Resources 295

Chapter 10 Questions 295

Chapter 10 Answers 295

Index **297**

Intro

Thank you for purchasing my book! Since I doubt many readers indulge elaborate intros I'll keep this short and sweet. Luckily for you the organization of this book was given much forethought. Each chapter builds sequentially on the material previously discussed and topics are introduced at a moderate pace--this allows readers to absorb the material quickly but not be overloaded with information. You'll find the text sprinkled with analogies, detailed explanations, and what I would like to think witty humor. At the end of each chapter you'll be greeted by questions along with full solutions--there's no gated portal that extorts you for more money so take advantage of this. In addition, you can download the source code from each respective chapter on Github: https://github.com/purcellconsult/

If you like this book then awesome, I hope it lights a fire under you to take your programming new heights. If you discover any erratum or have suggestions on how I can improve this book then shush, keep it on the down low will you. Books are not that easy to write ;). In all seriousness email me at: purcellconsult@gmail.com

You won't get any monetary awards, not even Bitcoin, but you'll get my gratitude. Also, if you want to spy follow with me on social media then feel free to do so as I'm on there. I'm also available for corporate training in Java or agile software development. Below are website and social media details.

- Consultancy website: http://www.purcellconsult.com

- Instagram: https://www.instagram.com/purcellconsult

- Twitter: https://twitter.com/DougPurcell3

Happy coding!

- Doug Purcell

Chapter 1: The fast guide to running your first java program

Before we download anything let's explore what happens under the hood when a program is executed in Java. Having a firm understanding of these concepts will help you to make sense of the compiling and running phases once we get to it.

Under the hood

The Java platform is a combination of the application programming interfaces (APIs) and the Java Virtual Machine (JVM). The **Java APIs** are libraries of pre-tested code that programmers can utilize to speed up development. The Java programs are interpreted by the JVM which is software that mimics a machine's processor. The reason why mimic is used is because it's abstract rather than physical hence the word *virtual* in its name. The specification describes an **instruction set,** or the portion of computer architecture that relates to programming. It includes native data types, registers, memory architecture, interrupts, exceptions, and information about the opcodes. An instruction set could also be classified as the interface between a computer's software and its hardware.

The JVM runs on top of an operating system. When a program has successfully compiled it's converted into byte code which the JVM can interpret. The JVM cannot interpret a plain java file which is why it must be compiled first. Once converted, this file can now be run on a variety of machines without the need for re-compilation. This is the power of the JVM and is also one of the selling points of Java which is *write once and run everywhere*. No need to panic if the above didn't make sense to you. It should become clearer once we learn how to download and configure Java on our machine.

The components

There are several components we need in order to successfully write and execute our first Java program. We need the Java Development Kit (JDK) which is available in both 32-bit and 64-bit format. The *bit* refers to the way that a computer processor or CPU handles information. In layman terms, a 64-bit OS handles larger amounts of Random Access Memory (RAM) better than a 32-bit OS. If you're on a Windows operated machine then an easy way to find out if you're running a 32 or 64-bit OS is to locate Windows search and type in the text "system."

Below is a screenshot of my OS:

System

Processor:	Intel(R) Core(TM) i5-4210U CPU @ 1.70GHz 2.40 GHz
Installed memory (RAM):	4.00 GB
System type:	64-bit Operating System, x64-based processor
Pen and Touch:	Touch Support with 10 Touch Points

Most computers developed in the early 90s used a 32-bit OS but modern computers tend to use a 64-bit OS. At the time of publication the latest version of the Java product is Java 8. The full name for Java 8 is "Java Platform Standard Edition 8" which is commonly abbreviated to Java SE 8. Its associated products are Java SE Development Kit 8, abbreviated to JDK 8, and Java SE Runtime Environment 8, which is abbreviated to JRE8.

The first step we should to take is to download JDK 8 which you can access on Oracle's website:

```
http://www.oracle.com/technetwork/java/javase/
downloads/jdk8-downloads-2133151.html
```

The JDK is a bundle of tools that allows coders to build Java programs. The JDK is not equivalent to the JRE. The JDK can be considered a superset of the JRE because the JRE is bundled inside the JDK. In other words, you don't need to download the JDK and JRE separately as the JRE is already included with the JDK. Inside the JRE is a module called the Java Virtual Machine (JVM) which executes programs line-by-line and is also known as the *interpreter*.

Every platform that's compatible with Java has their version of a JVM. Inside the JVM is a module called Just in Time Compiler (JIT)–this refers to the compilation done during runtime and is when the byte code is translated into machine code. When a Java program is compiled into byte code it's not directly executable, which is why this additional step is needed. Java Standard Edition Platform contains two implementations of the JVM which is the Java HotSpot Client VM, and Java HotSpot Server VM. These are designed to increase the performance when running applications on the client or server side. An example of a type of user that may want to download just the JRE is a business person who just needs to run a Java program to use, but has no desire to do any development.

The tools that you will be using for compiling and running Java files are executables which can be found in the bin directory of your JDK download. After you download the JDK the next step is to set the system path.

Setting the system path

After you have installed the JDK you can start compiling and running Java programs right off the bat. If you downloaded the JDK as normal then the default location for javac is at the following path: C:\Program Files (x86)\Java\jdk1.8.0_60\javac

To compile a file named `FeelsGood.java` you would type the following into command prompt:

`"C:\Program Files (x86)\Java\jdk1.8.0_60\bin\javac"`
`FeelsGood.java`

However, by setting the system path you can avoid the hassle of writing out that long ugly path.

Below are the steps on how to do this on a Windows operated machine.

Find Windows search and then type in the text "advanced system settings" and you should see a dialog box up like in the below screenshot:

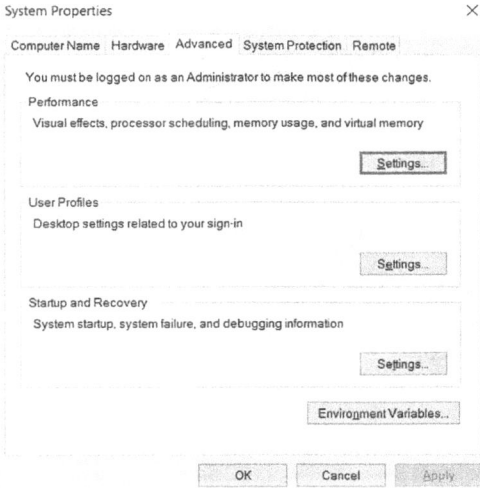

Next, click the Environment Variables button and under the System Variables section locate the Path field and click edit. A dialog box should appear which allows you to add the path to the environment variable. Assuming that you didn't change the default download location of the jdk, it should be located at: `C:\Program Files (x86)\Java\jdk1.8.0_60\bin\`

Click the OK button and close remaining dialog boxes. Once your system path is set, it's time to test that everything works correctly. You can open up the command prompt on Windows by hitting the Windows key + R, and then type cmd to run command prompt. It should look like the screenshot below:

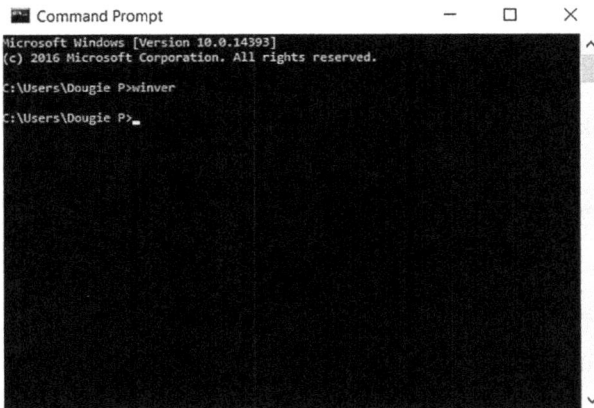

Type the text javac in command prompt. If installed correctly it should spit out a bunch of options like in the following screenshot.

```
■■ Command Prompt                          —    □    ✕

Microsoft Windows [Version 10.0.14393]                          ^
(c) 2016 Microsoft Corporation. All rights reserved.

C:\Users\Dougie P>winver

C:\Users\Dougie P>javac
Usage: javac <options> <source files>
where possible options include:
  -g                         Generate all debugging info
  -g:none                    Generate no debugging info
  -g:{lines,vars,source}     Generate only some debugging info
  -nowarn                    Generate no warnings
  -verbose                   Output messages about what the compiler is doing
  -deprecation               Output source locations where deprecated APIs are u
sed
  -classpath <path>          Specify where to find user class files and annotati
on processors
  -cp <path>                 Specify where to find user class files and annotati
on processors
  -sourcepath <path>         Specify where to find input source files
  -bootclasspath <path>      Override location of bootstrap class files
  -extdirs <dirs>            Override location of installed extensions
  -endorseddirs <dirs>       Override location of endorsed standards path
  -proc:{none,only}          Control whether annotation processing and/or compil
ation is done.                                                  v
```

If it hasn't been configured correctly it will say something like `javac is not recognized as an internal or external command, operable program or batch file.`

If this occurs then the culprit is that you didn't set the path correctly. Make sure that you know the precise path of the jdk on your machine. If you downloaded the jdk as normal then the file should be located at this location on your Windows machine: `C:\Program Files (x86)\Java\jdk1.8.0_60\bin\`

Find the file, click it, hold down the shift key and then right-click and select "Copy as path." Once that's done edit the environment variables by pasting the path. If you forgot the location in which you downloaded the jdk to then you'll have to do the unthinkable and locate the saved file. Luckily, Windows have a search option near the taskbar that allows you to search for documents on your system.

To check the version of jdk you have installed type the following in command prompt: javac –version

The output should be similar to this: `javac 1.8.0_60`

To check the version of Java you have type this in command prompt: java –version.

The output should be similar to this:

`java version "1.8.0_65"`

`Java(TM) SE Runtime Environment (build 1.8.0_65-b17)`

`Java HotSpot(TM) Client VM (build 25.65-b01, mixed mode)`

Note, ignore the "1" in front of the version number. You know that this is a flavor of Java 8 due to the 8.0 in it.

Writing your first java program

Before you can write your first program you need more tools. Java can be typed in a simple text editor such as a Notepad on Windows, Gedit on Linux, or TextEdit on OS X. You could alternatively download an integrated development environment (IDE) which includes features for speeding up development time. They typically include a source code editor, debugger, build automation, and code completion features. If you're new to programming then my advice would be to skip the IDEs and stick with simple text editors until you start building more larger and complicated programs.

Once you decide which editor or IDE you prefer go ahead and open it. We're going to pay homepage to a classic R & B song called "Feels Good" by singer Tony! Toni! Toné!

The program is going to print the following text to the console: *It feels good, yeah!*

Step one: Declare a class

In your editor type the following snippet of code at the very top:

```java
public class FeelsGood {

}
```

Java is an object oriented programming (OOP) language, and classes are a fundamental part of it. Every Java program must declare a class. If the class name is one word then the first word should be capitalized by convention. If the class name includes more than one word then the first letter of the second word should also be capitalized and so on. The class declaration should have an open and closing curly brace ({ }). The rest of the code most be contained within these curly braces or an error will manifest during compilation.

Step two: Create the main method

Every Java application must have at least one main method. This is true if it contains just one class, or 10,000 classes. The main method is the entry point to the Java program and tells the compiler where to start. Copy the following snippet of code in between the class declaration:

```java
public static void main(String [] args) {

}
```

This snippet of code will make sense more sense once you learn about access modifiers, methods, strings, and arrays in the future chapters. However, in the meantime go ahead and memorize it because you will be writing it often.

Step three: Add the print statement

The last step for writing the Java program is to include a print statement which will print the text to the screen. Paste the following snippet in between the main method:

```
System.out.println("It feels good, yeah!");
```

The complete program should look like the following:

Figure 1.0

```
public class FeelsGood {

public static void main(String [] args) {

System.out.println("It feels good, yeah!");

}

}
```

Step four: Save the file

Once you finished typing the program go ahead and save it somewhere with the name FeelsGood.java. It's critical that the filename matches the class name or less an error will occur during compilation.

Step five: Change into the directory of your Java file

Once you confirmed that everything is correct, open command prompt, and change into the directory that your Java file is located. You can change up a directory by using the cd keyword. For example, if you saved your Java file in your Desktop, then you can change into the Desktop directory by using the following command: cd Desktop.

Step six: Compile the Java file

To compile a Java file use the following syntax: javac FileName.java. In this case the specific syntax will be javac `FeelsGood.java.` If compilation is successful no error messages will appear.

Step seven: Run the java file

After successful compilation it's time to run the file. If you were to check in the same directory in which you compiled your file, you should notice an associated .class file for it which in this case will be `FeelsGood.class.` This .class file contains the byte code that the JVM will execute line-by-line. To run the program type the command: `java FeelsGood`

The following message should be printed to the terminal: "It feels good, yeah!"

If the message is printed then congratulations! You have successfully written your first Java program and this is the first of many that you'll do in this book. Below is an image that illustrates the relationship between the JDK, JRE, and JVM when you compile and run a Java program.

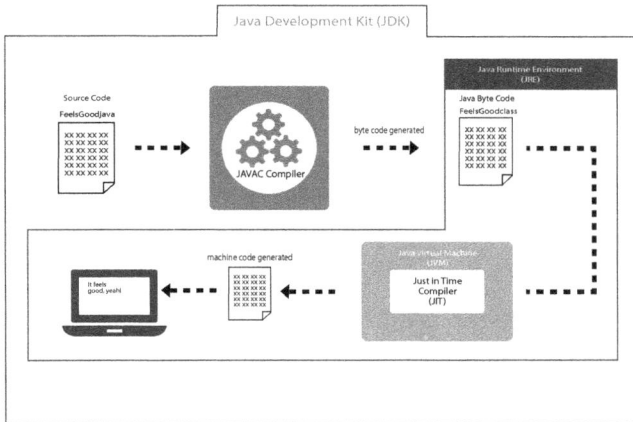

99 problems but my first program ain't one!

If were unable to run your first Java program then no worries; you're not the first person to experience this. Below are solutions depending on the context of the error. Debugging is a common occurrence in the daily life of a programmer so it's important to be able to think critically in order to resolve issues timely.

Compiler errors

`'javac' is not recognized as an internal or external command, operable program or batch file`

How do you interpret this weird jumbo of text? What this means in plain English is that javac (the compiler) is not recognized therefore Windows cannot locate it. To correct this you should edit your path variable so that javac can be invoked from any location. For steps on how to do this refer back to the Setting the system path section of this chapter.

Syntax errors

These are the type of errors that manifest if you incorrectly type something in your program. Java like all programming languages has a set of rules that are strictly enforced in order for a program to successfully compile. The Java compiler will typically provide the type of error, the line it occurred, and the position of the error within the code. Paying close attention to these hints will help you eradicate syntax errors timely.

Here's an error that's caused by having a different class name from the file name:

```
FeelsGood.java:1: error: class Feelsgood is public,
should be declared in a file named Feelsgood.java

        public class Feelsgood {
            ^
```

1 error

Here's another syntax error caused by incorrectly typing System.out.println:

```
FeelsGood.java:5: error: package system does not exist

        system.out.println("It feels good, yeah!");
            ^
```

1 error

If you're getting errors like these then review Figure 1.0 line-by-line and verify that your program matches it exactly. This goes from the case type, spacing, curly braces, and semi colons. Also, make sure that the class name matches the file name, and that the file name has a .java extension.

Semantic errors

The syntax of a language refers to the combination of symbols that creates a valid structured document. The semantics are concerned with deriving meaning from the elements in a program. A program can be syntactically correct but semantically incorrect. A famous example of this is by linguist Noam Chomsky who said that "colorless green ideas sleep furiously" in his 1957 book *Syntactic Structures*. This sentence is syntactically correct but is simply bonkers! All languages have a grammar, which is used to verify that a sentence has been constructed correctly.

A common semantic error in Java is: `error: variable a might not have been initialized.`

This occurs when a local variable has not been initialized but is being used in the program. This will make more sense once you have covered the material about access modifiers in chapter four.

Runtime errors

These types of errors manifest when the program is run. For example, if you can compile a program but it crashes during runtime then you got yourself a runtime error. These can be quite difficult to track at times. An example of a runtime error is division by 0 or reading in a file that doesn't exist.

```
Error: Could not find or load main class FeelsGood
```

This means that Java was looking for FeelsGood.class but couldn't find the associated .class file. The solution is to make sure that you compiled and run the Java file in the same directory. You can ensure that the .class file is in the same directory as the .java file by typing the text dir in command prompt. This lists all of the files in a directory in alphabetical order.

If you can't find both files in the same directory then try re-compiling the .java file. If it compiles without errors then the associated .class file should appear in that directory.

Chapter 1 Re-factored

In this chapter you discovered all of the steps required to install and run your very first Java program. Below is a condensed recap of the steps involved.

Download and run the JDK

To find the appropriate version of jdk for your operating system visit this page on the Oracle website here: http://www.oracle.com/technetwork/java/javase/downloads/index-jsp-138363.html

Update the path to the system variable

To access this area on a Windows powered OS, follow these steps: Click start->control panel, Double click on System and select Advanced system settings. Next, click the "Environment Variables" button and under the "System Variables" section locate the Path option and click edit.

Test your configuration

To test that you have configured the system variable correctly open command prompt and type javac. The command line interface should appear and display several options after you hit Enter. If you get an error then the system variable wasn't set correctly. Re-trace your steps and ensure that the path to the system variable is correct.

The steps to compile and run a Java program are as follows:

1) Open command prompt

2) Change into the directory of your java file by using the cd command

3) Compile the file by using: javac FileName.java

4) Run the file by using: java FileName

Chapter 1 Resources

Integrated Development Environments:

Eclipse (Windows, Linux, OS X, Solaris): `https://eclipse.org`

NetBeans (Windows, Linux, OS X, Solaris): `http://netbeans.org`

BlueJ(Windows, Linux, OS X, Solaris): `http://www.bluej.org`

IntelliJ (Windows, Linux, OS X, Solaris): `https://www.jetbrains.com/idea`

Text Editors:

Notepad++ (Microsoft Windows): `https://notepad-plus-plus.org`

Sublime Text (Windows, OS X, Ubuntu): `https://www.sublimetext.com`

Vim (UNIX, Mac, Ms-Windows): `http://www.vim.org`

Atom (Windows): `https://atom.io`

Emacs(GNU/Linux, Windows, OS X): `https://www.gnu.org/software/emacs`

Updating the PATH variable for Solaris and Linux operating systems: `https://docs.oracle.com/javase/tutorial/essential/environment/paths.html`

Chapter 1 Exercises

1) T or F: The Java development kit (JDK) and the Java runtime environment (JRE) physically exist. The JVM does not.

2) T or F: The Java Runtime environment contains tools for compiling and run-

ning a Java application.

3) T or F: Only the JRE could be considered a subset of the JDK.

4) T or F: The JDK is in reality a bundle of tools for developing Java programs.

5) T or F: The Java compiler converts filename.java into byte code which has an associated .class file.

6) T or F: The JDK is available for Windows, OS X, Linux, and Solaris operating systems.

7) T or F: Java source code is compiled into byte code which is architectural neutral object code. The object code is then interpreted by a Java Virtual Machine.

8) T or F: Javac is the java compiler. It compiles java source code into byte code.

9) T or F: The Java Virtual Machine (JVM) interprets and translates byte code into native machine language. The JVM is the same for every operating system which makes Java portable.

10) T or F: The Just in Time Compiler (JIT) compiles the byte code into machine code at runtime before executing it. Heavy optimizations are done during this period to increase performance.

11) T or F: When a java file is compiled, the byte code can be executed directly.

12) T or F: The JRE has two virtual machines which are Client and Server.

13) Which of the following is true about the java programming environment? Select all that apply.

    a) It's a programming language

    b) It's an API specification

    c) It's a virtual machine specification

    d) All of the above

14) The JVM supplies which of the following. Select all that apply.

    a) Class loader

    b) Compiler

    c) Garbage collectors

    d) Runtime libraries

15) T or F: A syntax error is a type of compile time error.

16) T or F: A type of compile time error is a semantic error.

17) T or F: A type of runtime error is a semantic error.

Chapter 1 Answers

1) True. If you downloaded and installed the JDK you will find folders for the JDK and the JRE but not one for the JVM since it's an abstract machine.

2) False. It contains tools for running a Java program but none for compilation.

3) False, both the JRE and the JVM is considered subsets of the JVM.

4) True. Those tools can be discovered inside the bin folder of the jdk. Some of these tools include javac which is for compilation, java which is the standard application launcher, and jdb which is a debugger tool.

5) True. If a file is successfully compiled an associated .class file will be created for it.

6) True.

7) True.

8) True.

9) False. While the JVM interprets byte code, every operating system has its own implementation of it.

10) True.

11) False. It's not directly executable in the byte code format. It must be converted into the native machine code before it can be executed which is the job of the JVM.

12) True.

13) Choice (d) is correct.

14) Choices a), c), and d) are correct.

15) True. Syntax errors are discovered during compilation.

16) True. Some semantic errors can are detected at compile time. For example, trying to use an uninitialized local variable is a semantic error.

17) True. A semantic error can be a compile time or runtime error.

Chapter 2: The insider guide to java primitive types

There are two primary data types in Java which are primitive and reference types. This chapter will start with the most basic one which are primitive types—these data types store values which can be manipulated throughout the program. Java has 8 primitive types which are byte, short, int, long, floating point, double, boolean, and chars. In this chapter we'll do an in-depth exploration of all of the primitive types so that we can start incorporating them into our programs.

Integrals

In school we learned about the number line which is a way to pictorially display numbers. Many types of numbers can be represented on it such as integers and natural, whole, rational, and real numbers.

The integral data types In Java are interested in only in integers. Integers in mathematics include numbers in the set of negative infinity to positive infinity. It can be represented in set notation as: {...-3,-2,-1, 0, 1, 2, 3...}.

In computers there's something known as memory which is where information is stored. Every time a data type is added to a Java program, memory from the computer is consumed. However, not all data types are created equal. Some data types can hold a wider range of numbers and therefore consume more memory when they're allocated. Even though some data types can hold very large numbers like the long data type, no data type can hold an infinite size of numbers due to memory constraints on a computer.

For example, we can calculate large numbers like the following on a piece of paper:

96,373,893,939,393,993,939

+   6,373,399,393,939,393

However, this is not possible by using primitive types because there's none that support integers this large. Remember, numbers are data, and data eats up memory on a computer. If a program consumes too many resources then that could lead to performance issues. Primitive data types represent a finite set of numbers, and each data type has a specified range.

byte

Imagine that you're in a restaurant with some friends, and you're friend offers to share some food with you. You can take a small bite if you're curious to see how the food tastes. In this context a small byte can be interpreted as a small parcel of whatever it is. The byte is the smallest integral data type in Java and has a range from $2^7 - 2^7$-1, or -128 … 127. In layman terms, the smallest value a byte can store is -128, and the maximum value it can store is 127. Going over the predefined data range of ANY primitive type will cause your program to generate compilations errors or behave in unexpected ways. To create bytes in Java use the following syntax:

```
byte a = 100;
```

short

This is the second smallest integral data type in Java, and its name is a good indication of this. Short data types can hold data within the range of $-2^{16} - 2^{16}$-1, or -32768… 32767. Therefore, the smallest value that this data type can hold is -32768, and the largest one it can hold is 32767. To create shorts in Java use the following syntax:

```
short b = 1000;
```

int

The keyword int is abbreviation for integer, and this type is far more common than byte and short. The int data type can hold integers in the range of $-2^{31}…2^{31}$-1 or -2147483648 to 2147483647. To create integers in Java use the following syntax:

```
int c = 20000;
```

long

Just think of the `long` primitive type as a bigger and badder version of the `int` data type. It can do anything that an integer can but better hence its name. The data range for the long is $2^{63} - 2^{63}-1$ which translates to -9.223372e+18...9.223372e+18. To create longs in Java use the following syntax:

```
long d = 350000000;
```

char

Have you ever visited a foreign website and saw text and symbols that you weren't accustomed to seeing? Every wondered how this was made possible? The answer is with the assistance of Unicode. To make a long story short Unicode is a computing industry standard that encodes, represents, and handles text from most of the world's writing systems. The project was founded circa 1980s and the purpose of it was to create a universal character set so everyone, regardless of their national boundaries could encode characters in their native language on a computing device. There are so many languages that have been discovered, and there's potentially more waiting to be unearthed.

The latest version of Unicode at the time of publication is Unicode 9.0 which encodes over 128,000 characters. Java uses UTF-16 which is one of the most popular versions of Unicode.

The syntax for declaring a char in Java is listed below:

```
char x = 'A';
```

You can also input a character's representative Unicode number in your Java program with the following syntax:

```
char example = '\uUnicodeNumber';
```

This is how it would look in a Java program:

```
char x = '\u00A3';
```

The output of this would be: £

Chars must be enclosed within the apostrophe symbol or less your program will generate a compile error.

Chars in Java take up two bytes in memory, and are unsigned as they only store positive numbers. The range for chars in Java is 0 – 65,535.

Floating point types

In the previous section we learned about integral types which are numbers which can be expressed as integers. Now we're ready to learn about the other type of numbers which are floating point types—these are numbers which are represented in fractional notation such as .55, 3.14159, etc. Another way to look at it is that integral types store only integers, while floating point types store real numbers. In mathematics, real numbers include integers, rational numbers, and irrational numbers. Note imaginary numbers are prohibited in Java which is why dividing by 0 causes an error. Java uses the most common implementation of floating point types which is IEEE 754.

float

The first type of floating point is a float which is a 32-bit IEEE 754 floating point. It's not recommended to use floating point types in a program in which accuracy is a top priority, like a financial application. The data range for floating point types are 1.40129846432481707e-45 to 3.40282346638528860e+38.

Here's the syntax for how you can declare a variable of type float in Java:

```
float x = 0.5f;
```

The letter f is needed as this denotes that it's a float. You'll need to put f to explicitly tell the compiler "hey, even though this number contains a decimal, I want you to treat it as a float."

If you don't put f then Java will interpret this as a double by default and will generate an error. A double is the second kind of floating point.

double

A double is like a float except that it has a wider range. The range for a double in Java is 4.94065645841246544e-324d to 1.79769313486231570e+308d. Below is the syntax for how you can declare a double:

```
double x = 0.5;
```

Notice the difference between how the double is declared compared to that of the float? The double doesn't need a special letter because double is the default type for declaring decimals in Java.

Booleans

Booleans are a simple data type which can only accept two values: `true` or `false`. In computers, the number 1 represents true, and 0 represents false. Don't let the simplicity of `booleans` deceive you as they're very powerful. For example, `booleans` can be used inside conditional statements which control the flow of program execution. You'll learn more about that in the next chapter. Here's how you declare a `boolean` in Java:

```
boolean e = true;
```

Figure 2.0: Table of 8 Primitive Data Types

Name	Description	Range
byte	8-bit signed two complement	-128...127
short	16-bit signed two complement	-32,768...32,767
int	32-bit signed two complement	-2,147,483,648... 2,147,483,647
long	64-bit signed two complement	-9,223,372,036,854,775,808... 9,223,372,036,854,775,807
float	single point precision	1.40129846432481707e-45... 3.40282346638528860e+38 (+ or – numbers)
double	double point precision	4.94065645841246544e-324d to 1.79769313486231570e+308d, (+ or – numbers)
boolean	1-bit.	0...1
char	unsigned Unicode UTF-16	0...65,535

Painless guide to binary, octals, and hexadecimals

In grade school we learned how to count and then we translated these skills to the outside world such as counting money when making a purchase. For example, if you go to the gas station to purchase a $1 ticket to play the power ball, but only have change for $10, the simple calculation of $10 - $1 is done and you are returned $9. You can perform all sorts of calculations in your head such as 10 + 5, 56 – 11, 6 × 7, and so on. You're doing calculations based on the decimal number system, which has a radix of 10. In mathematics, a **radix** is how many digits are used in the number system which is listed below:

{0,1,2,3,4,5,6,7,8,9}

With these ten numbers you perform computations in order to manipulate the digits. Numbers can be manipulated to carry out many useful applications. For example, numbers are used in order to create telephone numbers, serial numbers, ISBNs, to tell time, and calculate the amount of people that attend a music festival.

Numbers are useful mathematical objects and the decimal number system, also known as base 10, is one of the many number systems in existence. There are surprisingly a plethora of number systems in the world, and some of them may blow your mind. For example, Oksapmin is a language spoken by the natives in Telefomin District, Sandaun, Papua New Guinea which utilizes a base-27 number system! To make things even more interesting they use their entire body to count. The Georgian numeral system is a combination of base-10 and base-20 as the numerals from 30-99 uses base-20. Now that we know that there are many ways to represent numbers, let's focus our attention on the number systems for computing.

Binary numbers

Let's take a look at the number 1084—do you agree that it could also be written as $1 \times 1000 + 8 \times 10 + 4 \times 1$? The answer is yes because those numbers will equal $1000 + 80 + 4 = 1084$. This is base 10 which means all numbers can be represented in powers of 10s. Let's look at another example like say15, 262? How would you represent this in power of 10s?

To convert a decimal in powers of tens follow these steps: Start at the digit that's farthest to the right. In this case it's a 0. Next, multiply that digit by 10^0, which is 2×1 or 2. Increment the power of ten by one each subsequent multiplication and multiple that by the digit. So, the next one should be 6×10^1, then 2×10^2, then 5×10^3, then 1×10^4. This equals $10,000 + 5,000 + 200 + 60 + 2$ which reduces to 15,262 which means the conversion was done correct.

The process is similar for binary numbers but instead of using powers of 10 we're using powers of 2. Instead of having a radix of 10 like decimal does, binary have a radix of two, which are the digits 0 and 1. The bit farthest to the right in a binary string will be 2^0, and it increments by one each subsequent digit. Here's a chart of the first 12 binary numbers:

2^0	2^1	2^2	2^3	2^4	2^5	2^6	2^7	2^8	2^9	2^{10}	2^{11}	2^{12}
1	2	4	8	16	32	64	128	256	512	1024	2048	4096

To convert a decimal into binary you must represent it in power of 2s, and then place a 0 or 1 at the appropriate bit. Java uses twos complement which allows programmers to perform arithmetic operations on positive and negative integers. The other option is unsigned integers which only allow operations on positive numbers. Chars are an example of a data type in Java that uses this. Let's do some experimentation shall we. Let's represent binary numbers in 4-bit twos complement.

0 can't be represented in powers of 2s. Therefore, it translates to 0000 binary.

1 represented in power of 2s would be 2^0. This translates to 0001 in binary.

2 represented in power of 2s would be 2^1. This translates to 0010 in binary.

3 converted into power of 2s would be $2^1 + 2^0$. This translates to 0011 in binary.

4 converted into power of 2s would be 2^2. This translates to 0100 in binary.

5 converted into power of 2s would be $2^2 + 2^0$. This translates to 0101 in binary.

6 converted into power of 2s would be $2^2 + 2^1$. This translates to 0110 in binary.

7 converted into power of 2s would be $2^2 + 2^1 + 2^0$. This translates to 0111 in binary.

8 converted into power of 2s would be 2^3 or 1000 in binary. But wait, there's a problem. The maximum value that can be stored in 4-bit twos complement is 2^3-1 which is equal to 7. That means that the binary string of 1000 can't be a positive number. It's actually a negative number because the range for 4-bit twos complement is $-2^3...2^3$-1, or of the set [-8, 7]. Note, if the bit farthest to the left is a 1, then that denotes that the integer is a negative number in signed two complement. Otherwise, it's a positive integer.

The formula for representing a negative integer over n-bits in twos complement is as follows:

1. Represent the positive form of the number in binary. For example, 4 in binary is 0100.

2. Take the complement of the binary string. This means to invert the bits. The result is now 1011.

3. Add one to the inverted bit. To add bits in binary is the same as adding digits in decimal. You sum the numbers as normal and carry any numbers that's greater than or equal to the radix. For example, in decimal notation numbers greater than or equal to 10 are carried. For example, if the sum of two numbers is ten then the 1 is carried. In binary, two is carried by placing 1 bit down and carrying the other. Here's the result of adding 1 to 1011.

    11

   1011

+ 0001

———

  1100

Therefore, -4 represented in 4-bit twos complement is 1100.

Let's learn how to store a binary String in a Java program. To store binary bits in Java you'll need to use the prefix 0b followed by the binary digits. For example, to translate 127 into binary would be the following:

```
byte x = 0b01111111;
```

In addition, java allows you to add the underscore in order to separate digits. For example, the following is permissible as of Java SE 7 and later:

```
byte x = 0b0111_1111;
```

You can also capitalize the b in the prefix so that it displays 0B. It simply boils down to the programmer's preference.

Octals

Octals is another number system used in computing that as its name indicates is base 8. It has a radix of [0, 7]. Here's a table for the first 8 squares of 8.

8^0	8^1	8^2	8^3	8^4	8^5	8^6	8^7	8^8
1	8	64	512	4096	32768	262144	2097152	16777216

Let's practice some conversion, convert 8 into octal. The integer 8 can be represented as 8^1 or 0010_8. The underscore 8 denotes that it's octal. To input this into a java program the digit farthest to the left should be a 0. Below is an example of how to input the integer 8 into octal in Java.

```
byte x = 0010;
```

Note, for octal you can place an underscore after the 0. For example, the following is legal and won't generate any errors:

```
byte x = 0_0011; // prints 9
```

The above syntax is not permissible with bytes or hexadecimals. For example, 0b_0000_0011 would generate an error for illegal underscore.

Solve this fun riddle in your free time: Oct 31 = Dec 25.

Hexadecimals

Hexadecimals are more widely used than octals; some examples in which they're used are color references and addresses in memory. Hexadecimal is radix 16, but if you dissected the word, hexa means six in ancient Greek. However, why does the word contain a prefix that means six when there are 16 numbers in the system? The first ten hexadecimal integers are 0-9, and the next six use the letters A-F. Below is a listing for hexadecimals:

1

2

3

4

5

6

7

8

9

A = 10

B = 11

C = 12

D = 13

E = 14

F = 15

Seeing letters that represent numbers may throw you for a loop at first, but keep in mind that it's a number system and who ever invents it can decide what encoding scheme to use. A number system could encode $ as 10 or # as 15 if they wanted.

Let's convert 10010 into hexadecimal.

The answer would be $16^1 * 6 + 16^0 * 4 = 0x0064$. To create a number in hexadecimal format use the 0x prefix. For example, here's how you declare a hexadecimal in Java.

```
int x = 0x0064;
```

You can also capitalize the x in the prefix if you wish so that it will read 0X.

What's $FFFF_{16}$ converted into decimal? The answer is $16^3 \times 15 + 16^2 \times 15 + 16^1 \times 15 + 160 \times 15$ which equals = 65,535. Note, you cannot store a hexadecimal in a byte or octal, it must be stored in an integer or less the compiler will throw an error.

For a side note hex color codes are used on web pages. For example, #FFFFFF is white, #FF0000 is red, and #000000 is black.

Literals

A literal is the representation of explicit values in a Java program. Integers, floating point types, chars, and booleans all have literals.

Integer literals

Java makes it easy for you to enter integers in a myriad of formats. For example as you learned previously you can enter an integer in byte, octal, hexadecimal, or decimal notation. Let's look at the following snippets of code:

a) `byte a = 100;`

b) `short b = 500;`

c) `int c = 1000;`

d) `int d = 0b1111_1111;`

e) `int e = 0_5757_5757;`

f) `int f = 0xABC_DEF;`

In **a** the literal is 100, in **b** the literal is 500, in **c** the literal is 1000, in **d** the literal is `0b1111_1111`, in e the literal is `0_5757_5757`, and in f the literal is `0xABC_DEF`.

Floating point literals

Floating point literals are ones that can be represented as either a `float` or `decimal`. To represent a floating point literal as a float you must include a lowercase or capital F at the end of the number like in the following snippet:

`float x = 36373.8833F;`

In the above example, 36373.8833 is the floating point literal.

The below snippet of code is an example of a double floating point literal:

`double a = 5373.38373;`

The floating point literal in the above example is 5373.38373. Numbers of type `double` are the default floating point literals. However, if you want, you can put a lowercase or capital d to explicitly state that it's of type `double`. Below is an example code snippet:

```
double b = 002002.3D;
```

In addition, you can also declare floating point literals with the letter e which denotes raise to the power of. The letter e used in Java is different from the letter e found on a calculator which is known as Euler's number and is equal to 2.7182818 2845904523536028747113527. Look at the following code snippet:

```
double c = 5.6725789e5;
```

In the above example the floating point literal is 567257.89

Boolean literals

Boolean has two types of literals which is either true or false. Let's analyze some code for a better idea.

```
boolean isPessimist = false;
```

In the above example, false is the boolean literal.

```
boolean isOptimist = true;
```

In the above example, true is the boolean literal.

Char literals

A char literal is a single character that's enclosed within single quotes (' '). Look at the code snippet below:

```
char capitalA = 'A';
```

In the above example A is the char literal. As mentioned earlier, chars in Java use UTF-16 to encode characters. Therefore, the letter A could also be stored as its associated decimal number in UTF-16. The following code snippet shows how to correctly implement that in Java:

```
char dec65 = 65;
```

Operators

Operators in Java are symbols that manipulate **operands**. An operand is data in which an operation is being performed on. Operators are similar to functions, with the main distinction being that most programming languages don't allow programmers to create their own operators, but instead allow them to create their own functions. The list of operator features in a programming language vary from language-to-language and in this section we're going to analyze the myriad of operators available in Java.

Unary Operators Crash Course

Un is derived from Old English and means "one" and that's the perfect way to remember these type of operators as they only work on a single operand.

Plus (+)

The plus operator makes a number positive. It can be applied to integers or floating points. An example of it is listed below:

```
int positiveInt = +50;
```

Minus (-)

This is the opposite of the positive operator as it makes a number negative. The below code snippet shows the minus operator in action.

```
float negativeFloat = -62.2882F;
```

If a number doesn't have a plus or minus sign then it's assumed to be positive by default.

Increment (++)

There are two variations of increment operators which are pre-increment and post-increment. Below is the syntax and description for each variation:

Post increment

```
x++;
```

This returns the old value of x and then increments it by one.

Pre increment

```
++x;
```

This increments the value of x by one and then returns the new value.

Let's look at an example code snippet of the post increment operator in use.

int apple = 0;

```
apple = apple++ + 2;
```

This translates to apple = 0 + 2 which is three. Remember, post-increment means that the current value of apple is returned which is 0, and then it's incremented. Now, let's analyze a statement including the pre-increment operator.

```
int orange = 0;
```

```
orange = ++orange + 2;
```

The statement ++orange returns 1 and then adds that to 2 which makes orange equal to 3.

Decrement (–)

Similar to the increment operator there are two types of decrement operators which are the pre decrement and post decrement operators.

Post decrement

```
x--;
```

This returns the current value of x and then decrements it. Let's look at an example code snippet of the post increment operator in use.

```
int postDecrement = 1;
```

```
postDecrement = postDecrement-- + 2;
```

postDecrement-- returns 1 and then 2 is added to it. Therefore, this statement is evaluated as 1 + 2 which is three.

Pre-decrement

```
--x;
```

This decrements the value of x and then returns the new value. Let's look at this operator in action.

```
int preDecrement = 1;
```

```
preDecrement = --preDecrement + 2;
```

`--preDecrement` returns 0 and then two is added to it. Therefore, the statement is evaluated as 0 + 2 which is equal to 2.

Bitwise Complement (~)

The bitwise complement will only make sense if you understand binary numbers. What this operator does is invert the bits of a binary string. Let's look at the following code snippet:

```
byte negate = ~127;
```

When negate is printed the result will be -128. What? Let's break this down bit-by-bit (no pun intended). Convert 127 into binary which is: 0111-1111. Next, invert the result which will be1000-0000 or -128 in decimal.

Binary Operators Crash Course

The prefix for binary is bi, which is derived from the Latin word bis which means two. This is an excellent way to remember these operators as they operate on two operands. The type of binary operators in Java is arithmetic, equality, relational, conditional, bitwise, and bitwise shift.

Arithmetic

In grade school you learned arithmetic which is the branch of mathematics which involves manipulating numbers. The same principles that you learned then can be used to build sophisticated Java programs. In this section you'll gain an introduction to the various arithmetic operators in Java.

Addition (+)

You can add two operands by using the + symbol. Below is an example of this operator in action.

```
int sum = 36 + 7292;
```

The above result is 7328

Subtraction (-)

Java allows programmers to subtract two operands by using the minus (-) symbol. Below is an example of this operator in action.

```
int sub = 100-90;
```

The result is 10.

Multiplication (*)

Java allows programmers to multiply two operands by using the asterisk symbol (*). Below is this operator in action.

```
int mul = 10 * 10;
```

The above result is 100.

Division (/)

Java allows programmers to divide two operands by using the forward slash symbol (/). When dividing integers in Java the remainder is discarded. Below is an example of this operator in action:

```
int div = 10 / 3;
```

The above result is 3.

Below is an example of the division operator applied to a float.

```
float div = 10.5F / 3;
```

The above result is 3.5.

Modulus (%)

Java allows programmers to take the remainder of two operands by using the percent (%) sign. This operator works by diving two operands, and then returning its remainder. Below is an example code snippet of the modulus operator in action using two integers.

```
int mod = 5 % 4;
```

The result is one.

Below is an example of the modulus operator being used on floating points.

```
float mod = 5.5F % 4;
```

The above result is 1.5.

Assignment, Equality, Relational, and Conditional

These types of binary operators allow programmers to assign values or to compare two operands and return a value of type `boolean`.

Assignment (=)

This sets the value on the right to the variable on the left. Look at the following code snippet:

```
int a = 20;
```

The value of 20 is stored in the variable a of type `int`.

Equality

There are only two types of equality operators available in Java which are equal to and not equal to.

Equal to (==)

If you want to test if two operands are equal to each other use the equal to (==) operator. Be careful not to confuse this with the assignment (=) operator. The former assigns the value on the right to the variable in the left. However, the equal to operator uses two equal signs, and compares two operands. Look at the following code snippet:

```
int y = 20;

int z = 21;

boolean result = y == z;
```

The value of result is equal to `false` since 20 is not equal to 21.

Not equal to (!=)

This operator checks to see if two operands are not equal to each other. If they are different then the result will be true and false otherwise. Below is an example of this operator in action.

```java
double y = 20.3738;

double z = 20.3682299;

boolean result = y != z;
```

The above code snippet will return true since the two doubles are not equal.

Relational

The relational operators in Java compare the size of two operands.

Less than (<)

The less than operator compares the operand on the left to the one on the right. If the operand on the left is less than that on the right, then the boolean will evaluate to true--It's false otherwise. Below is a Java snippet using the less than operator.

boolean result = 3 < 5;

The result will evaluate to true.

Less than or equal to (<=)

The less than or equal to operator determines if the operand on the left is less than or equal to the one on the right. If at least one of those cases is true then the result will be `true`--it's `false` only if both of those conditions are not meet. Look at the following code snippet:

```java
boolean result = 5 <= 10;
```

The value of result when printed is true.

Greater than (>)

The greater than operator determines if the operand on the left is larger than the one on the right. If that's the case then true is returned, otherwise the result is false. Below is an example of the operator in action.

```java
boolean result = 5 > 10;
```

Since 5 is less than 10 `result` will return `false`.

Greater than or equal to (>=)

The greater than or equal to operator determines if the operand on the left is greater than or equal to the one on the right. If at least one of those conditions is true then the result is `true`--the result is `false` only if both of those conditions are not meet. Look at the following code snippet:

```
boolean result = 1.5 >= .1;
```

Even though 1.5 is not equal to .1, it's greater than it therefore `result` will return `true`.

Instanceof

This operator will become more lucid once you learn about objects in chapter four. Into the meantime just know that Java has two types of data types which are primitive types or the ones taught in this chapter, and objects which will be explained in chapter 4. The operator `instanceof` is used to compare an object of a certain type. Let's look at the following code:

```
String x = "hello";

boolean isTrue = x instanceof String;
```

The variable `isTrue` will return `true` since the variable x is an object of `String`.

Conditional

The conditional operators in Java are derived from logic and have a set of rules that determines if an expression is `true` or `false`.

AND (&&)

The AND (&&) operator evaluates to `true` if and only if both expressions evaluate to `true`. Below is a truth table that displays the situations in which the evaluation is `true` or `false`.

Figure 2.1: And Operator Truth Table.

A	B	&&
True	True	True
True	False	False
False	True	False
False	False	False

Below is a code snippet that uses the AND (&&) operator:

```
boolean result = ( 4 > 3) && (5 < 10);
```

The variable result stores the value true since 4 is greater than 3 and 5 is less 10. Let's modify the expression so it says this:

```
boolean result = ( 4 < 3) && (5 < 10);
```

The expression will evaluate to `false` since 4 is less than 3.

OR (||)

The OR operator evaluates to `false` only if both expressions are `false`. Below is a truth table that displays the situations in which the evaluation is `true` or `false`.

Figure 2.2: OR Operator Truth Table.

A	B	||
True	True	True
True	False	True
False	True	True
False	False	False

The below code snippet features the OR operator:

```
boolean result = ( 10 < 27.82) || (3.383 < 10);
```

The above statement evaluates to true. The left-hand portion of 10 < 27.82 evaluates to true and the right hand portion of 3.383 < 10 is `true` as well. Therefore, `result` evaluates to `true`. However, let's see what changes when the above statement is modified to state the following:

```
boolean result = ( 10 > 27.82) || (3.383 > 10);
```

The variable result will now evaluate to false since both the left-hand and right-hand side of the expression evaluates to `false`.

The logical operators of && and || enables short circuiting, which means that the right side is not evaluated or less it's needed. For example, in the expression (4 < 3) && (5 < 10), after the first portion of 4 < 3 is evaluated, the right hand portion of 5 < 10 is not since the && operator is used. With AND it only takes one expression to evaluate to `false` in order to determine that the result will be `false`.

Ternary or Conditional Operator (? :)

This operator is special as it has three operands. A way to remember this is that the prefix *ter* derives from Latin which means *thrice* or three times. What this operator does is assign a value to a variable based on how the `boolean` evaluates. If it evaluates to `true` then the variable is assigned to the first value, and if it's `false` then the variable will be assigned to the second value. Let's look at an example:

```
int result = (5 > 10) ? 5: 6;
```

The expression of 5 > 10 is evaluated to `false`. Therefore, the value of 6 is assigned to `result`.

Bitwise Operators and Bit Shifts

For programmers that have a background in C they may be familiar with the concepts of bit operators and shifts. For those who first programming language is Java they may find bit shifting Bizzaro World. Here's the lowdown about bit shifting. Computers love bits because 0s and 1s come natural to them, it's like their mother tongue. Therefore, they find manipulating them quite inherent. Computers can do all types of things with bits in rapid time that humans can only dream of such as ANDing, Oring, XORing, shifting, and inverting them. Let's explore the bitwise operators and shifts more.

Bitwise AND (&)

Bitwise AND (&) applies the AND operator to the individual bits of a number and returns the result. The below code snippet shows the & operator in action:

```
int a = 5 & 10;
```

The result of a is 0. To get a better idea of how this operator works we must convert 5 and 10 into binary and then evaluate each portion bit-by-bit. Here's the above expression converted and evaluated:

```
0101 & 1010 → 0000
```

Bitwise Inclusive OR (I)

Bitwise OR (|) applies the OR operator to the associated bits of an expression. Let's analyze the following code snippet:

```
int a = 5 | 10;
```

The result of a is 15. Here's the above expression converted and evaluated:

0101 & 1010 → 8 + 4 + 2 + 1 which is 15.

Bitwise Exclusive OR (^)

The Exclusive OR operator (^) commonly referred to as the XOR operator is an eccentric sounding operator. AND/OR are everyday words in the English language but it would be odd to hear the expression "work hard XOR go home." Let's analyze the truth table for this operator:

Figure 2.3: XOR Operator Truth Table.

A	B	^
True	True	False
True	False	True
False	True	True
False	False	False

Let's analyze a code snippet that applies the XOR operator:

```
int a = 5 ^ 10;
```

```
0101 ^ 1010 → 8 + 4 + 2 + 1 which is 15.
```

Logical and bitwise operators are not identical. A difference between them is that Logical AND includes short-circuiting while bitwise operators do not. Therefore, using bitwise operators is overkill in most situations and is rarely used in production code.

Left shift (<<)

The left shift operator shifts the operand by the specified number of bits to the left. If the integer is not in binary format then the integer is converted into binary, and the most significant bit (MSB) or the one farthest to the left will be shifted by the number specified. Let's look at an example for clarity.

```
int x = 5 << 2;
```

In the above example 5 is equal to 0101 in binary. When 5 is shifted two bits the result will be 010100 which equals 20.

Right shift (>>)

The right shift operator shifts the operand by the specified number of bits to the right. If the integer is not in binary format then the integer is converted into binary, and the least significant bit (LSB) or the one farthest to the right will be shifted by the specified number. Let's look at an example below:

```
6 >> 2

0b0110 >> 0b0010 = 0001, or 1.
```

Operator Precedence and Associativity

Before we start evaluating expressions we need to know the rules for operator precedence and associativity. Precedence is the rules that dictate which procedures to perform first, and is similar to the orders of operations in mathematics that we learned in grade school. For example, both multiplication and division has a higher precedence than addition and subtraction. Associativity describes how operators of the same precedence are evaluated in the absence of parenthesis. The following table lists operator precedence.

Table 2.4: Java 8 operators with precedence and associativity.

Operators	Precedence
postfix	x++ x--
prefix	++x --x +x -x ~ !
multiplicative	* / %
additive	+ -
shift	<< >> >>>
relational	< > <= >= instanceof
equality	== !=
bitwise AND	&
bitwise exclusive OR	^
bitwise inclusive OR	|
logical AND	&&
logical OR	||
ternary	? :
assignment	= += -= *= /= %= &= ^= |= <<= >>= >>>=

Binary operators excluding the assignment operators are left associative, while unary operators are right associative. Let's look at some examples to make more sense of this. The first one is listed below.

```
5 % 2 * 5
```

Will the expression be evaluated like 5 % (2 * 5), or will it be evaluated like (5 % 2) * 5? Refer to the table of Java operators. We can see that the modulus (%) and multiplication (*) operators are all on the same level and therefore have identical precedence. Therefore to determine how this operation is evaluated we turn to the rules of associativity which states that these binary operators are evaluated from left to right. Therefore, the expression is equivalent to (5 % 2) * 5 which equals 5.

Widening and Narrowing Conversions

Java allows primitives of one type to be converted to that of another type under certain conditions. When a primitive type of a smaller range is converted to a type of larger range this is known as widening conversion. For example, if you create a variable of type byte, and then assign it to another variable of type `int` this is a widening conversion because you're going from 8-bit to 32-bit. When a primitive type of a larger range is converted to a primitive type of a smaller range this is known as narrowing conversion. For example, when you have a variable of type `int` and then save it to a variable of type `short` then this is narrowing conversion. When using conversions it's important to know that data may be lost, so we'll explore some examples.

Widening primitive Conversions

Java permits 19 specific widening primitive conversions. The rules are listed below:

- `From byte to: short, int, long, float, double`
- `From short to: int, long, float, double`
- `From char to: int, long, float, double`
- `From int to: long, float, double`
- `From long to: float or double`
- `From float to double`

The widening primitive type conversion doesn't lose information of the magnitude in the following situations:

- From an integral type to another integral type
- From `byte, short, or char` to a floating point type
- From `int` to `double`

- From float to double via the strictfp expression (reserved keyword in java that restricts floating point calculations for portability reasons)

A widening conversion from int to float, long to float, or long to double may result in loss of precision, or in other words the result may lose some of its least significant bits of value. The new floating point value will be rounded to the nearest integer using IEEE 754 round-to-nearest mode. A widening conversion from float to double that doesn't use strictfp may result in data lost. The strictfp keyword cannot be applied to individual variables, but instead can be applied to classes, interfaces, and methods which are explained in chapters four and five.

Below are some examples of widening conversion in which no information is lost:

```java
byte a = 127;

short b = a; // widening conversion from byte to short

-----------

short c = 1000;

int d = c; // widening from 16-bit short to 32-bit int

-----------

char e = 126; // storing integer literal as a char

System.out.println(e); // prints the tilde character

-----------
```

One way to test that your primitive conversions doesn't result in any information loss is to subtract the converted variable from the original one. If no information is lost then the result should be zero. Look at the example below:

```java
int original = 2577889;

float copy = original;

copy = copy - original;

System.out.println("The result is " + copy);

-----------
```

The following is printed to the console: The result is 0.0

Therefore, no information is lost.

Narrowing primitive Conversions

Java permits 22 specific narrowing primitive conversions. The rules are listed below:

- `short to byte or char`

- `char to byte or short`

- `int to byte, short, or char`

- `long to byte, short, char, or int`

- `float to byte, short, char, int, or long`

- `double to byte, short, char, int, long, or float`

A narrowing primitive conversion may result in information lost of magnitude and precision. In order to do a narrowing conversion in Java you must use the cast operator which uses the following format: `(type)operand`

Below is an example of a narrowing conversion:

```
int a = 100;

byte b = (byte)a;

System.out.println(b);
```

The above prints 100 and there's no information lost since the maximum value for a `byte` data type in Java is 127, and 100 falls within the range. However, let's modify the above example so that it states the following.

```
int a = 150;

byte b = (byte)a;

System.out.println(b);
```

The result that's printed is now different. The maximum value that can be allocated to a `byte` is 127 but now with the forced conversion something has to give. When variable a is cast to a byte here's the binary representation: 10010110.

Remember, that in signed two's complement, if the most significant bit (MSB) is one then that denotes that the corresponding integer is negative. Therefore, the binary string converts to the following powers of twos: $-2^7 + 2^4 + 2^2 + 2^1 = -128 + 16 + 4 + 2 = -106$.

The following is an example of a floating point type being converted into a long:

```
double e = 2527272.228;

long f = (long)e;

System.out.println("Double e converted to long f is "
+ f);
```

The following is printed to the console: 2527272

Long is an integral type which means that it cannot store decimal values. Therefore, the mantissa or the decimal part of variable e (.228) is *truncated* or cutoff.

Variables in Java

Java provides a set of rules and conventions for creating variables. Violating these rules will generate compile errors. Naming conventions on the other hand are designed to make programs more understandable and easy to read. Nicely crafted variable names can provide programmers quick insights into what the code does. There are naming conventions for: variables, packages, classes, interfaces, methods, and constants.

The rules

There's a subtle difference between the term *identifiers* and *variables*. A variable is the storage location of data, while identifiers are the name of an element in a program. An identifier can be used to refer to variables, methods, classes, etc.

- Identifiers are case sensitive. For example, int a, is different than int A.

- Identifiers names can be of unlimited Unicode letters and numbers which means that super long identifiers are permitted. The following code snippet is a legal identifier even though I wouldn't recommend it:

  ```
  String supercalifragilisticexpialidocious;
  ```

- Identifiers can start with a letter, dollar sign ($), or underscore (_).

- Identifiers may not begin with a number. However, numbers may follow identifiers that begin with a letter, dollar sign, or underscore

- Whitespace is not allowed

- An identifier may not be the same as a reserved keyword in java.

Below is a listing of the reserved keywords in Java 8.

Figure 2.4: list of reserved keywords in Java 8

abstract	continue	for	new	switch
assert	default	goto	package	synchronized
boolean	do	if	private	this
break	double	implements	protected	throw
byte	else	import	public	throws
case	enum	instanceof	return	transient
catch	extends	int	short	try
char	final	interface	static	void
class	finally	long	strictfp	volatile
const	float	native	super	while

The following are examples of legal identifiers:

```
int $money;

int a1thing;

String _abc;

char $1;

byte _123;
```

The Conventions

Just because something is legal doesn't make a good choice! Below are the conventions you should follow when naming your identifiers:

- Always begin your identifiers with a letter.

- Never use dollar signs.

- Never begin your variable names with an underscore (_).

- Use actual words instead of esoteric characters. For example, `double calculateAverage()` is much more descriptive than `double x`.

- If your identifier is only one word then spell it out in all lowercase, otherwise capitalize the first letter of each subsequent word. For example, `int numberOfComputers,` and `double priceOfDinner` are examples of this convention.

- If the variable holds a *constant* or a value that won't change then by convention the identifier is in all caps and each word s separated by an underscore For example, `static final int HOURS_IN_DAY = 24;`

Comments

Java has three types of comments which are single line, multiline, and javadoc. All comments are ignored by the compiler and are there for programmers to help clarify the intent of the code. Avoid adding comments that are likely to become outdated and if your code requires many comments, then consider rewriting your code so that its more clear. Java comments can be formatted in four types of ways.

Single Line Comments

Also known as C++ style comments, single line comments are written on one line. Writing the text over multiple lines will cause an error.

The syntax for creating them is to use two forward slashes which is shown below:

```
// I will never be seen!
```

Multiline Comments

Also known as C-style comments are those that can be written over multiple lines. The syntax for creating this is as follows:

```
/* add text here */
```

An example is shown below:

```
/*    I like to move it, move it

      I like to move it, move it

      I like to move it, move it

      You like to

      (Move it!) */
```

Javadoc Comments

These comments look like multiline comments with the addition of one extra asterisk in the opening delimiter. These comments are special because they can be used to generate documentation comments for a program. The syntax for creating this is as follows:

```
/** add comments here */
```

Below is an example of a Javadoc comment:

```
/**     NOW this is the law of the jungle,
 * as old and as true as the sky,
 * And the wolf that shall keep it may
 * prosper, but the wolf that shall
 * break it must die. As the creeper that
 * girdles the tree trunk, the law runneth
 * over and back; For the strength of the
 * pack is the wolf, and the strength of
 * the wolf is the pack.
 * ~ Rudyard Kipling
 *
 */
```

Chapter 2 Re-factored

In this chapter you were introduced to a myriad of topics that will allow you to start building basic Java programs. You learned about the 8-primitive data types in Java along with how to manipulate them using various operators. You also learned how to create a variable, and their associative rules and conventions in Java. Primitive types and operators are a common occurrence Java programs. Therefore, mastering them is critical in order to write even basic programs. There's no escape from them, so committing to mastering them is critical for your future Java success☺.

Chapter 2 Resources

The latest version of Unicode: http://unicode.org/charts

IEE 754: http://grouper.ieee.org/groups/754/

How to write Doc Comments for Javadoc Tool: http://www.oracle.com/technetwork/articles/java/index-137868.html

Chapter 2 Exercises

What do the following expressions evaluate to when printed?

1. 5 − 2 * 3 + 4 / 5

2. 5 % 5 + 4 * 3 / 10 + 9

3. 5 / 9 / 8 / 7 / 6 + 5

4. 5 * 3 − (5 * (5 + 2) / 9)

5. Evaluate the following snippet of code.

   ```
   int a = 1;

   a++;

   System.out.println(a);
   ```

6. Evaluate the following snippet of code:

   ```
   int b = 1;

   ++b;

   System.out.println(b);
   ```

7. Evaluate the following snippet of code.

   ```
   int a = 5;

   int b = ++a + a++;

   System.out.println(b);
   ```

8. Evaluate the following snippet of code.

   ```
   int a = 1;

   int b = ++a * a++ / 5 + a++ / 6;

   System.out.println(b);
   ```

9. Evaluate the following snippet of code:

   ```
   int i = 1;

   i = i++ + 2 * i++ / 5 - 8 + i-- + --i;

   System.out.println(i);
   ```

10. Create a variable named average that sums the numbers 100 and 50 and then takes the average. Print the output to the console by passing the variable average to the method: `System.out.println()`.

11. Evaluate the following code snippet:

```
float x = 7.2828F;

++x;

System.out.println(x);

int y =(int) x;

System.out.println(y);
```

12. Evaluate the following code snippet:

```
double a = .0009;

a = a + .1;

System.out.println(a);
```

13. The weight of an object can be defined as the mass multiplied by gravity. The formula for this is w = mg. Since the weight is force, the Interactional System of Units (SI) can be described in Newton's. In freefall, gravity is equal to 9.8 Newton's/kg. Write an equation that calculates the weight of an object if its mass is known. The mass should be in kilograms.

Sample input:

```
double weight = 0.0;

double mass = 6;

double gravity = 9.8;
```

Sample output:

Weight of mass 6.0 is 58.800000000000004 Newtons

Chapter 2 Answers

1. Output: -1

    5 – 6 + 4 / 5

    5 - 6 = -1

2. Output: 10

    0 + 12 / 10 + 9 = 10

3. Output: 5

    0 / 8 / 7 / 6 + 5

    0 / 7 / 6 + 5

    0 + 5 = 5

4. Output: 12

    * 3 − (5 * 7 / 9)

    * 3 − 3 = 12

5. Output: 2

6. Output: 2

7. Output: 12

8. Output: 0

    2 * 2 / 5 + 3 / 6 = 0

9. Output: -3

    1 + 2 * 2 / 5 − 8 + 3 + 1 = -3

10. Output:

    ```
    int average =(100 + 50) / 2;
    System.out.println(average);
    ```

11. Output: 8.282801 and 8

12. 0.1009

13.
    ```
    public class Gravity {
      public static void main(String[] args) {
            double weight = 0;
            double mass = 6;
            double gravity = 9.8;
            weight = mass * gravity;
            System.out.println(weight + " newtons");
      }
    }
    ```

Chapter 3: Making a statement

They're all types of statements: fashion statements, income statements, and the list go on. The type of statements we're going to focus on in this chapter is the one that deals with java programming. In the previous chapter we learned about primitive types and operators, now we're going to take that a step further by using them to construct statements that can handle conditional flow and execute repetitive tasks.

Expressions, statements, and blocks

A Java program is comprised of expressions, statements, and blocks. Expressions are the combination of variables and operators that that are created in accordance to the syntax of a language and evaluates to a value. In English, a sentence can be terminated by a period, exclamatory mark, or question mark. In Java, statements are terminated by the semicolon (;). Statements can be thought of as being comprised of one or more expressions. Below are examples of expressions that are also statements:

```
int x = 5;

double piValue = 3.14159;

long bigNumber = 353782828L;
```

An expression can be a statement, but a statement can't be an expression--It's a one-way relationship. Java has an assortment of statements available. To declare a variable you'll use what's called a declaration statement. As the name suggests, it declares a variable by including its data type and name. For example, the following are examples of declaration statements in Java:

```
int winningNumber;

boolean isHealthyDiet;
```

In addition, it's legal to declare multiple variables of the same type on a single line in Java. For example the following are permissible:

```
int mostPopularNumber = 7, secondMostPopularNumber = 3,
firstPlace = 1;
```

However, declaring multiple variables on a single line could be difficult for other developers to follow. Therefore, to increase readability consider listing each declaration on a separate line.

Another kind of statement is **control flow** which regulates the order in which statements are executed. Control flow statements in Java are typically placed within opening and closing curly braces ({ }) which is known as a block of code--A block is a portion of code that's grouped together.

Below is an example of a block of code:

Figure 3.0: A block of code in Java.

```
{
  double listPrice = 100;

  double discountRate = .25;

  double salePrice = 0.0;

  salePrice = listPrice - (listPrice * discountRate);

  System.out.println("The new price is = " + "$" +

  salePrice);

}
```

As you can see, the curly braces help structure your code. However, they're not necessary in Figure 3.0 due to the linear flow of the code. What if you want the code to execute different blocks depending on how statements evaluates? A good start would be to use what's known as a conditional statement and group blocks of code together that can manipulate data accordingly.

if-then statement

A conditional statement alters the flow of a program contingent on how the boolean expression evaluates. In real life, if-then statements are used all the time. For example, if the student doesn't do their homework, then they will fail the assignment. If the worker doesn't come to work for a week then they will get fired. If the child doesn't behave then they will get coal for Christmas. I like to think of if-then statements as cause and effect relationships. Below is the syntax for an if-then statement.

```
if (condition is true) {

// execute statements

}
```

Let's dissect this blow-by-blow. The first portion of the if-then statement is this:

```
if (condition is true)
```

The if keyword is a reserved keyword in Java and must be included in order to create the if-then statement. Using the keyword in a different context such as a variable name will generate a compile error. The portion within the parenthesis or the condition is where the boolean expression goes. As mentioned in chapter two boolean expression is one that evaluates to true or false. The parenthesis in the condition is needed as excluding it will generate a compile error. Examples of boolean expressions are as follows:

```
5 + 6 == 11; // true

0 % 5 != 0; //  false

(5 * 3) < 10 && (5 % 2) < 12 || (5 + 3) < 20 // false
```

The last portion of the if-then statement is the body:

```
{
// execute statements

}
```

The body or the block of statements enclosed within the curly braces is executed if the boolean evaluates to true. If the boolean is evaluated to false then the statements within the body are ignored and the control of the program exits out of the body of the if-then statement. Let's put everything together that we just learned. What happens when the following code is evaluated?

Figure 3.1: If-then statement demo in Java.

```
if (5 % 2 == 1) {

  System.out.println("Whoop Whoop!");

}
```

The condition of 5 % 2 ==1 is first evaluated. In chapter two we learned about primitive types and how to evaluate them which makes mastering conditional logic easier. The expression is evaluated from left-to-right since that's the modulus operator's associativity. Since 5% 2 is executed first and has a remainder of 1, the condition evaluates to `true`. Therefore, the body of the if-then statement is executed and `Whoop Whoop!` is printed to the screen.

if-then-else statement

The if-then-else statement is an extension of the if-then statement. You'll use the if-then statement if you want to execute a block of code if a condition evaluates to `true`. You should use the if-then-else statement if you want to provide multiple control paths. Here's the syntax for the if-then-else statement:

```
if (condition is true) {

 // execute statements

} else {

 //execute statements

}
```

As you can see, the structure is identical to the if-then statement with the extension of one piece of code which is the `else` block.

The flow of execution will make it to the `else block` only if the boolean expression evaluates to `false`. If it does, then the statements within the `else` block is evaluated and flow of execution exits out of the else block. That's it! The else block can be thought of as the block of code that's executed by default if the boolean expression evaluates to `false`. Let's take a look at some code. What's the output of Figure 3.2?

Figure 3.2: If-then-else statement demo in Java.

```
if (5 % 2 > 1) {

 System.out.println("Whoop Whoop!");

} else {

 System.out.println("I'm as busy as a one-legged cat in
 a sandbox!");

}
```

The output is: `I'm as busy as a one-legged cat in a sandbox!`

The program first checks the boolean condition `if (5 % 2 > 1)`. Since 5 % 2 is equal to 1, the boolean evaluates to `false` because 1 is not greater than 1.

Therefore, the program jumps to the else block and executes the code which is to print the southern idiom.

Note, in this example the curly braces are not mandatory since the body contains a single statement. Therefore, the following code snippet will compile without any errors:

```java
if (5 % 2 > 1)

  System.out.println("Whoop Whoop!");

else

  System.out.println("I'm as busy as a one-legged cat in
  a sandbox!");
```

However, even though they're not needed doesn't mean that no future issues may manifest by not having it. For example, if you're working with a team and someone adds an extra statement to the `if` block, then the program will behave in unexpected ways. For example, let's look at figure 3.3 which builds on figure 3.2 by adding an additional print statement:

Figure 3.3: If-then-else statement demo with missing curly brace.

```java
if (5 % 2 > 1)

  System.out.println("Whoop Whoop!");

System.out.println();

else

  System.out.println("I'm as busy as a one-legged cat in
  a sandbox!");
```

Here's the unwelcoming message the compiler gives: `error: 'else' without 'if' else.` This is the compiler way of saying that they found the else keyword but it's missing an associated `if`. One solution to fixing this problem is to add curly braces. The updated code snippet is listed below:

```java
if (5 % 2 > 1) {

  System.out.println("Whoop Whoop!");

  System.out.println();

} else {

  System.out.println("I'm as busy as a one-legged cat in
  a sandbox!");

}
```

else-if

The if-then-else statement can again be extended with the addition of `else-if`. Below is the syntax for it:

```
if (condition is true) {
  // do this
} else if (condition is true) {
  // do this
} else if (condition is true) {
  // do this
}
.

.

else if (condition n is true) {
  // do this
} else {
  // do this
}
```

Here's the above syntax translated into layman terms. If this is true do this, if not exit out of the block and pass control to the next condition. If that is true do this, if not then exit out of that block and do this. Each subsequent condition is checked if the previous one evaluates to false. If all conditions evaluate to false then the else block is executed. Note, the `else` block is optional. Include it if it's needed but otherwise it's not mandatory. Let's explore an example to get a better idea of how to implement the `else-if` statement.

Imagine that you're an instructor and are in charge of creating a class. The school has a strict grading policy that's fixed across all subjects. Below are the grading guidelines:

A+ = 96-100

A = 93-95

A- = 90-92

The text `ring` is printed to the console.

This example could be converted into an if-then-else statement to replicate the same logic. Some developers prefer if-then-else statements while others prefer switch. My advice is to get comfortable with both so you can use whichever one is ideal for a task.

Looptopia

Have you ever done something monotonous and just thought to yourself that there has to be a better way? For example, imagine that you had a homework assignment in which you had to sum the numbers one through ten. This is an easy task, you can pull out a piece of paper, write out the numbers, and perform the arithmetic on it and bam and you're done.

However, what if the instructor asked you to sum the numbers from one through 100? This can be a tedious task, but it's doable and will just be busy work. What if the instructor asked you to sum numbers 1…1000 and to show each summation along the way? For example, $1 + 2 = 3$, $3+3 = 6$, $6+ 4 = 10$, all the way up to 1000? What was once a simple task just became annoying, but luckily problems like these are easily solved by a computer with the right type of code.

What you need is known as a loop, which is a sequence of instructions that repeats until a condition is meet. If a loop doesn't have a condition that terminates then what you get is an infinite loop which will keep repeating from *here to eternity*. Java offers four types of loops which are do while, while, for, and enhanced for loop. The latter is a loop that's reserved for iterating over an arrays, enums, and Collections which will be discussed in later chapters.

do while

Have you ever thought to yourself to do something while you were in the process of doing something else? This is in essence the idea behind the `do while` loop. Below is its syntax:

```
do {
  // statements
}
while (condition is true) {
  // statements
}
```

With a do while loop the first block of code is executed at least once and then the boolean in the condition is evaluated. The statements within the do block will keep executing while the boolean expression is true. Below is an example that we dissect.

Figure 3.5: Do while loop demo.

```
int i = 1;
do {
  System.out.println(i);
} while (++i <= 100);
```

Blow-by-blow analysis: The do block is executed by default which prints the value of i which is 1. The control flow passes to the while loop which pre-increments i and then evaluates if it's less than or equal to 100. While this is true the control flow of the program passes to the do block and then iterates or repeats until the condition is false which terminates the program. The next type of loop that we'll discuss is the while loop which is similar to do while except that it excludes the do portion.

while loop

An example of a while loop in everyday language is "while the computer is on, I will code Java." The syntax for a while loop is listed below:

```
while (condition is true) {
  // execute statements;
}
```

Here's an example of a while loop.

Figure 3.6: A while loop demo.

```
int i = 0;
while (i <= 300) {
    if (i % 2 == 0) {
        System.out.println(i);
    }
    i++;
}
```

Blow-by-blow analysis: The condition in the while loop is checked and since the initial value of i which is 0 is less than or equal to 300, the flow of the program passes to the if condition. Since i % 2 satisfies the condition, 0 is printed, and then the flow of the program passes on to the next line which increments i. This process repeats until the while condition is invalid, which is when i has the value of 301.

for loop

The syntax of the for loop is indicated below:

```
for( initialize counter ; check condition; update counter) {

// statements

}
```

The beginning of the loop can accept three expressions inside the parenthesis. Below is an explanation of each argument.

- Initialize the counter triggers the beginning of the loop. It keeps track of the number of iterations in the loop.

- In the second part of the for loop the boolean expression is checked. The for loop will continue for as long as the boolean evaluates to true. It will terminate once it evaluates to false.

- The counter is updated after the completion of each cycle. The counter is typically incremented or decremented.

Below is an example of a for loop.

Figure 3.7: A for loop demo.

```
for (int i = 10; i > 0; --i) {

    System.out.println(i);

}
```

Blow-by-blow analysis: The initialization is the first thing that's done, and the variable i is set to 10. The control flow then passes to the condition which is i > 0. Since this is true, the control then passes to the next portion which decrements i. Once that's done the control then passes to the body of the loop which prints i. The program then goes back to the beginning of the loop and the process repeats until the condition is terminated which is when i is equal to 0. The following is printed to the console: 10 9 8 7 6 5 4 3 2 1

Notes on the For Loop

Did you notice that the variable i is declared within the for loop? This type of variable is known as a local variable which means that it only exists within the block that it was created in. If you don't need the variable outside the scope of the for loop then it's a good idea to create it within the initialization phase.

The variables i, j, and k are typically used by programmers to indicate control within a for loop, but you can use any legal identifier you wish. Declaring them within the initialization portion will limit their lifespan and thus could potentially reduce errors.

The three expressions inside the for loop are optional. For example, this is perfectly legal in Java:

```
for (;;) {

  // statements

}
```

However, this will result in an infinite loop.

Also, curly braces are not needed if the body of a loop contains a single statement. However, I touched basis on this topic previously when discussing if-then-else statements. The choice to include or exclude them simply boils down to the preference of the developer.

Nested loops

All loops can be nested, or placed within the body of another loop. For example, the following is permissible in Java.

```
while () {

  while () {

    // statements

  }

}
```

The following syntax is also allowed:

```
for () {

  for () {
```

```
  // statements
 }
}
```

In addition, you can nest different types of loops. For example, the following is legal in Java:

```
while () {
 for () {
  // statements
 }
}
```

Nested loops are more common than one may think. For example, the odometer on a car is an example of several nested loops. Also, some websites have a visitor counter widget which is another example of a nested loop. Nested loops can be thought of as an action within an action. For example, let's assume that you have 3 boxes of cookies, and each bag contains five cookies. Here's the process that you will take if you were going to devour them all.

Open box #1

```
 Eat cookie 1
 Eat cookie 2
   .
   .
   .
 Eat cookie 5
```

Open box #2

```
 Eat cookie 1
 Eat cookie 2
   .
   .
   .
 Eat cookie 5
```

Open box #3

```
Eat cookie 1

Eat cookie 2

  .

  .

  .

Eat cookie 5
```

This can be translated into Java as follow:

```java
for (int boxNumber = 1; boxNumber <= 3; boxNumber++) {
    for (int cookieNumber = 1; cookieNumber <= 5;
    cookieNumber++) {
        eat(cookieNumber);
    }
}
```

The outer loop controls the inner loop. Once the outer loop runs, the inner loops repeat until its condition fails. The control then passes back to the outer loop and the process resumes. Inner loops typically iterate much faster than the outer loop. Let's take a look at an example to get a better idea.

Nested while loop example

Figure 3.8: A nested while loop demo.

```java
int i = 0;
while (i <= 2) {
    int j = 0;
    while (j <= 3) {
        System.out.println("i = " + i + " " + "j = "
        + j);
        j++;
    }
    i++;
}
```

Blow-by-analysis: Int i is initialized outside of the loop, and then is used in the first condition which is (i <=2). Since the condition is `true`, the statement `int j = 0` is executed and then the flow is passed to the second loop which is `while ( j <=3 )`. The statement is printed, and then `j` is incremented. The flow then passes to the next line which is `i++`. The flow then passes back to the outer loop and the entire process repeats two more times.

The output is as follows:

```
i = 0 j = 0

i = 0 j = 1

i = 0 j = 2

i = 0 j = 3

i = 1 j = 0

i = 1 j = 1

i = 1 j = 2

i = 1 j = 3

i = 2 j = 0

i = 2 j = 1

i = 2 j = 2

i = 2 j = 3
```

Note, the first loop is known as the outer loop while the second loop is known as the inner loop. The outer loop controls the inner loop, as once the outer loop terminates the inner loop does so as well. In addition, notice that `int i` is set outside of both loops. The scope of this variable can transcend past the loops. In other words, it can be used in the lines following the loops. However, `int j` was made within the loop, and is known as a local variable so its scope is limited to the blocks in which it was defined. For example, printing j outside the loop block will cause a compile error.

Nested for loop example

Figure 3.9: A nested for loop demo.

Here's an example of a nested for loop.

```
for (int i = 1; i <= 12; i++) {

    for (int j = 1; j <= 12; j++) {

        System.out.println(i + "x" + j + " = " + i *
        j);

    }

}
```

Blow-by-analysis: The outer loop sets the bounds of the loop which is from 1 through 12. Since the boolean is `true`, the control flow passes to the inner loop. The inner loop is a replica of the outer loop except that it's using a different variable which is `j`. The print statement then executes which will happen twelve times for each execution of the outer loop. The result will be the multiplication tables for the numbers 1...12.

break

Here's an easy way to remember the gist of a `break` statement. When you're tired and exhausted, say as a result of a very intensive workout, you may think to yourself "I need a break!" When you do this you depart from the routine you were doing. This concept is analogous to a `break` statement in Java. Break statements are used to terminate loops and switch statements.

For example, look at Figure 3.10:

Figure 3.10: A break statement demo.

```
for (int i = 1; i < 6; i++) {

    if (i == 3) {

        break;

    } else {

        System.out.println(i);

    }

}
```

This prints 1 and 2. The loop exits once the condition `i==3` is meet so the rest of the loop is not reached since the control flow has passed outside of the `for` loop once the `break` statement has executed.

continue

Have you ever played a video game and had to press a button to continue since the boss has zapped your health bar? The annoying boss caused a brief interruption in your gaming, but once you continue you can get back to the fun. This is analogous to how the `continue` statement works in Java. It interrupts the flow by forcing the next iteration of the loop to take place. Any code in between this is swiftly ignored. Let's take a look at the following example which is identical to the previous one except for a `continue` statement replacing the `break` statement.

Figure 3.11: Continue statement demo.

```java
for (int i = 1; i < 6; i++) {

    if (i == 3) {

        continue;

    } else {

        System.out.print(i + " ");

    }

}
```

The output is: 1 2 4 5

Once the condition `i==3` is reached the `continue` statement executes which pushes the control flow back to the beginning. Therefore three is not printed while the rest of the loop resumes as normal.

Chapter 3 Re-factored

In this chapter you were introduced to the wonderful world of statements in Java. Statements provide a myriad of benefits t such as allowing you to manage control flow and executing repetitive tasks in seconds. You learned about the different types of if-statements, along with the switch statement which can mimic the functionality of an if-then-else statement. You also learned about the various looping statements in Java and how they differ. If you're new to programming then take the time to go through the exercises. If you're having difficulties reaching a solution then try and break the problem into small manageable chunks and give it your best try. If you struggle then don't worry, as Rome wasn't built in a day. All written solutions for the exercises are provided following each chapter, and the associated source code for the problems can be found at: `https://github.com/purcellconsult/sourcecodelibrary-/tree/master/BookSource/ChapterThree`

Practice diligently and good things will happen.

Chapter 3 Exercises

1)   T or F: If a Java program has seven open curly braces then it should have seven closing ones.

2)   T or F: An if-then statement does NOT need an `else` block.

3)   T or F. An if-then-else statement must include an `else` block.

4)   T or F: If-then-else statements don't need curly braces if each block includes at most one statement each.

5)   T or F: Relational operators can be used inside the boolean expressions of conditions.

6)   T or F: The boolean expression of `true` is represented in the computer as 0.

7)   T or F: The logical operator (&&) and the bitwise AND operator (&) are equivalent.

8)   T or F: The code snippet of `x + 2` is a statement.

9)   T or F: You must use indentation in the code blocks of conditionals statements.

10) T or F: The logical expression of `!!true` evaluates to `true`.

11) T or F: An if-then else statement needs an `else if`.

12) T or F: A `while` loop needs an associated opening and closing brace or less the compiler will generate an error.

13) T or F: A `for` loop always needs curly braces even if the statement is just one line.

14) T or F: The `do-while` and `while` loop are logically equivalent. You can use anyone depending on which one you prefer.

15) T or F: An expression is the equivalent of a statement.

16) T or F: The following is an example of a statement: `i % 2`

17) Refer to the code snippet below:

```
int i = 5;
        int j = 10;
```

```
                int k = 15;
                if (i < 9)
                    if (j > i)
                        if (k > 20)
                            System.out.print("Hey");
                System.out.print("You!");
                System.out.print("Wanna Code?");
```

Which of the following is printed?

a) HeyYou!Wanna Code?

b) You!

c) You!Wanna Code?

d) None of the above

18) Are these two statements logically equivalent?

a)
```
int i = 0;
if (i > -5 && i < 2) {
  System.out.println("Life would be so much easier
  if we " +
  "only had the source code.");
}
```

b)
```
int i = 0;
if (i > -5) {
  if (i < 2) {
        System.out.println("Life would be so much
        easier if " +
        "we only had the source code.");
  }
}
```

19) What will the following print?

```
int i = 1;
if (i / 1 != 1 && ++i == 2) {
        System.out.println("Bonsai!");
}
```

20) A compile error occurs in the following code. What's the problem?

```
int i = 1;
if (i == 1) {
  i = 5;
} else {
  i = 5 * 5;
}
if (i > 0) {
  System.out.println("i is a positive number");
} else {
  System.out.println("i is a negative number");
}
if (i > 0 && i < 4) {
  System.out.println("i is between 0 and 4");
} else {
  System.out.println("recheck the conditions");
}
  else if (i > 4 && i < 8) {
  System.out.println("i is between 4 and 8");
}
```

21) There's an issue with the following snippet of code. What is it?

```
int i = 1;
```

```
if (true) {
  i = -1;
}
if (false) {
  i = 2;
}
}
```

22) There are two things wrong with the following snippet of code. What are they?

```
int i = 1;
if (true) {
  i = -1;
} else if (false) {
  i = 2;
} else {
  i = 0;
} else if (i < 2) {
  i = 3;
}
if (i > 5) {
  i %= 2;
} else {
  i = 0.5;
}
```

Write code that satisfies the following statements. Remember, in interval notation a square bracket [ ] denotes inclusive, or to include the end-values, while a round bracket ( ) denotes exclusive or to not include the end values.

23) Write an if-then statement that tests if an integer x satisfies this interval (0, 5).

24) Write an if-then statement that tests if an integer x satisfies this interval [-5, 5].

25) Write an if-then statement that tests if an integer x satisfies this interval (-7, 7].

26) Write an if-then statement that tests if an integer x satisfies this interval [-2, 20).

27) Write an if-then statement that tests if an integer x satisfies this interval [3, 4).

28) Write an if-then statement that satisfies this inequality for an integer x: – 6 >= x > 10

29) Write an if-then statement that tests if an integer x satisfies this interval [2y + 2, 10).

30) T or F: Assume that x, y, and z are real numbers.

- If x >= y, and y >=z. We can conclude that x is >= z.

- If x <=y, and y <=z. We can conclude that x <= z.

31) T or F. Assume that x and y are real numbers.

- If x is >= y, than y is greater >= x.

- If x is <= y, than y <=x.

32)

a) Write an `if-then` statement that test to see if a person can legally have a beer in the United States. In the US the drinking age limit for beer is 21. Use `legalDrinkingAgeInUS` as the identifier for the drinking age limit, and use `personAge` as the identifier that stores the person age. If the person is of the legal drinking age limit then print "Cheers!" to the console.

b) Extend the previous code so that it includes an `else` condition when the Boolean is false. The statement should say: `"Patience is bitter, but its fruit is sweet."` Jean–Jacques Rousseau.

c) Extend the previous code so that we are now checking to see what country someone is from, and if they're of the legal drinking limit of that country. The countries, their legal age drinking limit, and the message to print depending on the situation are listed in the table below:

Figure 3.12: Legal drinking age limit by country. LegalDrinkingAgeLimit.java.

Country	Legal drinking age	If user can drink	If user can't drink
United States (US)	21	Cheers	Sorry!
Ethiopia (ET)	18	T'chen chen	Yiqirta
France (FR)	18	à votre santé	Pardon
Germany (DE)	16	Prost	Es tut uns leid
Japan (JP)	20	Kanpai	Gomen'nasai
Mexico (MX)	18	Salud	Lo siento
United Kingdom (GB)	18	Cheers	Sorry

Translate the above table into a Java program using conditional statements. Here's a hint to how I solved it. I took a variable called, customMessage of type String. For a reminder, Strings allow you to store multiple characters together. This is how I declared it:

```
String customMessage = "";
```

This means that `customMessage` holds a String that has nothing in it. Here's the conditional block I made to verify if someone is an American and if they're of the legal drinking age limit:

```
if(personCountry == "US" && personAge >= 21) {

    customMessage = "cheers";

}
```

Fill in the remaining portions of the code.

33. Is the while statement needed for a `do while` loop? For example, will the following compile in Java without any errors?

```
do {

  i++;

}
```

34. Can you nest a for loop inside the do statement? For example, while the following code snippet compiler or result in an error?

```
int i = 1;

do {

  i++;
```

```
}
for (i = 0; i <= 10; i++) {

  System.out.println(i);

}
```

35. What does the following code print?

```
int i = 1;

int j = 0;

do {

        i++;

        System.out.println(j);

} while (i < 10);

{

        j = i - 1;

}
```

36. Write a do while loop that prints the statement "numbers of days in a common year" ONCE and then proceeds to print the numbers 1-365.

37. What's wrong with the following loop? Update the code so that the errors are removed.

```
int i = 1;

while (i < 10) {

        System.out.println(i);

}
```

38. What does the following code print?

```
int i = 1;

while (i <= 5) {

        i++;

        System.out.println(i);

}
```

39. How many iterations will be in the following loop?

    a)

    ```java
    for (int i = 1; i <= 10; i++) {

            for (int j = 1; j <= 7; j++) {

            }

    }
    ```

    b) Update the code so that you add a variable of type int called count that increment with each execution of the loop. Print the count outside of the loop.

40. Repair this loop.

    ```java
    for (int i = 0; i < 7; ++i) {

            if (i == 5) {

                        break;

            } else {

                        continue;

                    System.out.println(i);

    }
    ```

41. Is there a difference between what's printed in loop a vs. loop b?

    ```java
    Loop a:
    for (int i = 1; i < 11; i++) {

            System.out.println(i);

    }
    Loop b:
    for (int i = 1; i < 11; ++i) {

            System.out.println(i);

    }
    ```

42. What does the following loop print?

    ```java
    int i = 1;

    while (i != 13) {
    ```

```
        i++;
        System.out.println(i);
}
```

43. Are loops a and b equivalent? Why or why not?

```
Loop a:
int i = 1;
while (i != 13) {
        i++;
        System.out.println(i);
}
Loop b:
for (int i = 1; i != 13; i++) {
        System.out.println(i);
}
```

44. What does the following loop print?

```
int i = 1;
int j = -3;
for (;;) {
        if (i < 5) {
                System.out.println(i);
                i++;
        } else {
                System.out.println(j);
                j++;
        }
        if (i == 5 && j > 10) {
                break;
        }
}
```

45. What does the following code print?

```java
int i = 1;
int j = 1;
do {
        System.out.print("i = " + i + " ");
        i++;
} while (i < 6);
{
        System.out.println();
}
do {
        System.out.print("j = " + j + " ");
        j++;
} while (j < 5);
```

46. Write a program that prints the Unicode characters from the exclamatory mark (!) all the way to the tilde (~). Use `System.out.print()` instead of `System.out.println()` to do this so that the characters are displayed horizontally instead of vertically. Below is the output that you should get:

```
!"#$%&'()*+,-./0123456789:;<=>?@ABCDEFGHIJKLMNO
PQRSTUVWXYZ[\]^_`abcdefghijklmnopqrstuvwxyz{|}~
```

Hint. Use a Unicode character table so that you will know the correct UTF-16 codes to put in your program.

47. a) Write a loop that in the interval [1, 20] that prints the square of itself. For example, the square of 1...5 should be printed like the following:

1*1 = 1

2*2 = 4

3*3 = 9

4*4 = 16

5*5 = 25

b) Modify the loop so that it prints the squares of the following interval: [1,100].

48. Write a loop that prints the following pattern:

```
*

*  *

*  *  *

*  *  *  *

*  *  *  *  *
```

49. Write a loop that prints the following pattern:

```
OOOOO

OOOO

OOO

OO

O
```

50. Write a loop that prints the following pattern:

```
J****

*A***

**V**

***A*

****!
```

51. Write a loop that prints the following pattern:

```
XOXOXO

XOXOXO

XOXOXO

XOXOXO

XOXOXO

XOXOXO
```

52. Write a loop that prints the following pattern:

XXXXXX

XXXX

XX

X

53. Write a loop that prints the following pattern:

$ $ $ $ $

$ $ $ $ $

$ $ $ $ $

$ $ $ $ $

Hint: You can use the \t escape sequence to create a tab space between each $ symbol printed.

54. Write a loop that prints the following pattern:

XOOOO

XXOOO

XXXOO

XXXXO

XXXXX

55. Write a loop that prints the following pattern:

X X ▪ 2 1

X X ▪ ▪ 2 1

X X ▪ ▪ ▪ 2 1

X X ▪ ▪ ▪ ▪ 2 1

You can generate a square by using this Unicode number: u25a0.

56. Write a loop that prints the numbers between 1 and 2, and that increments by .15 each iteration.

57. Fibonacci numbers is a popular integer sequence in which the first two numbers of a sequence is defined, and the subsequent integers are the sum of the two previous ones. Fibonacci numbers have various applications in computer science such as Fibonacci cubes, Fibonacci heap data structures, and Fibonacci search technique. In addition, it's such a studied field in mathematics that it has a scientific journal dedicated to it called *Fibonacci Quarterly*. If that wasn't interesting enough Fibonacci numbers can also be found in nature such as in the arrangements of pineapple, artichoke, and aloe.

Here's the recurrence relation for a Fibonacci number: $F_n = F_{n-1} + F_{n-2}$.

The initial values are $F_0 = 0$, and $F_1 = 1$.

Write a loop that prints the first 14 Fibonacci numbers which are:

0, 1, 1, 2, 3, 5, 8, 13, 21, 34, 55, 89, 144, 233.

58. A geometric series in mathematics is a type of series that has a ratio between two successive terms. A famous series is known as Zeno's dichotomy, which can be represented in the form below:

$$\sum_{i=1}^{n} \frac{1}{2^i} = \frac{1}{2} + \frac{1}{4} + \frac{1}{8} + ...$$

Write a program that prints the first 10 terms of the series in fractional format.

Here are the first 10 terms:

$$\frac{1}{2} \quad \frac{1}{4} \quad \frac{1}{8} \quad \frac{1}{16} \quad \frac{1}{32} \quad \frac{1}{64} \quad \frac{1}{128} \quad \frac{1}{256} \quad \frac{1}{512} \quad \frac{1}{1024}$$

Chapter 3 Solutions

1. True. The number of open curly braces must equal the number of closing curly braces or less an error will generate.

2. True. You can write an if-then statement in Java without including the `else` block.

3. True. An if-then-else statement is an extension of the if-then statement and needs the `else` block to handle what to do next if the first condition evaluates to `false`.

4. True. While adding curly braces may make your code more readable, they're not mandatory if each block has one statement.

5. True. Examples of relational operators are >, <, and !=.

6. False. It's represented as a 1.

7. False. The logical operator is used in boolean expressions while the bitwise operator is used to manipulate individual bits.

8. False. An example of the code modified so that it would become a statement is `i = i + 2`.

9. False. While indentation will make your code more readable, the code will still compile without errors if indentation is skipped.

10. True. The exclamatory mark indicates the logical complement operator, and having two of them is a double negation. Therefore, the expression evaluates to `true`.

11. False. Java allows programmers to create an if-then-else statement with the option to add multiple `else if` blocks. The `else if` feature is available but not mandatory.

12. False. If the `while` loop has a statement that's just one line then it does not need any curly braces.

13. False. Like the while loop, the curly braces will be optional if the for loop contains a single statement.

14. False. They're not logically equivalent. For example, the statements in a `do while` loop are executed within the body of the `do` block. Then, the control flow passes to the `while` statement which is terminated with a semicolon. In a `while` loop the boolean expression is evaluated and the statements are executed within the `while` block until the condition is terminated.

15. False. While they're some overlap they are still some differences. For example, a statement can be thought of as multiple expressions, while the reverse is not true.

16. False, it's an expression. If the code was modified to `i %=2`, then it would be classified as a statement.

17. Choice (c). This is a good example of why having curly braces is a good idea even if it's not mandatory for the code to compile. The first two conditions are `true`, but the last condition is `false`. Therefore, the first print statement is ignored and the last two print statements are executed.

18. Yes, both code snippets will evaluate to the same value. The difference between them is that version `a` is a compound condition as it combines two booleans. In snippet `b` the conditions are separated—therefore, the first

if-statement validates that the first condition is `true`. Since it is the control flow passes to the next if-statement which again checks to see if the condition is `true`. Since it is then the statement executes. Version a is more readable.

19. Nothing. The condition `i / 1 != 1` is false since i is indeed equal to one. Therefore, the second condition is not evaluated due to short-circuiting, and the control flow passes outside of the body of the condition. Unfortunately, Bonsai! is not printed.

20. The `else if` statement comes after an `else` statement which should not be the case as it can only follow an `if` statement. To fix the problem convert `else if` to `else`. In this way the last block of code will execute by default if all of the prior statements evaluate to `false`.

21. The last curly brace is not needed. The number of open curly braces should match the number of closing curly braces. If there's a mismatch in the open vs. close curly braces then the following compile error will occur: `error: class, interface, or enum expected.`

22. What causes the first error is the portion below:

```
else if (i < 2) {
i = 3;
}
```

The compiler will say something like this: `error: 'else' without 'if'.` The `if` statement should come before the `else if` statement. One way to think of it is that the `else` block concludes the previous statements. Therefore, if an `else if` follows an `else`, then that would cause a compile error because it's continuing from nothing.

The second error is a result of this snippet here:

```
else {
i = 0.5;
}
```

The identifier `i` was declared as an `int`, but the code is storing a floating point type which is not permissible without an explicit cast. This is an example that's purely academic as you shouldn't see things like this in production code.

23. if(x > 0 && x < 5)

24. if(x >= -5 && x <= 5)

25. if(x > -7 && x <= 7)

26. if(x >= -2 && x < 20)

27. if(x >= 3 && x < 4)

28. if(x <= -6 && x > 10)

29. if(x >= 2*y + 2 && x < 10)

30. True. This is correct. This is also known as the transitive property of inequalities.

31. False. If x is >= y, then we know that y can only be less than x, or at most y can be equal to x. However, it's impossible for y to be greater than x with these conditions. The same logic applies to if x is <= y. This is known as the converse property of inequalities.

32.

a)

```
int legalDrinkingAgeInUS = 21;

int personAge = 21;

if (personAge >= legalDrinkingAgeInUS) {

      System.out.println("Cheers!");

}
```

b)

```
int legalDrinkingAgeInUS = 21;

int personAge = 20;

if (personAge >= legalDrinkingAgeInUS) {

      System.out.println("Cheers!");

} else {

      System.out.println("\"Patience is bitter, but
      its fruit " +

          "is sweet.\" Jean-Jacques Rousseau");

}
```

c)

```
String customMessage = "";

String usCountryCode = "US";

String ethopiaCountryCode = "ET";

String franceCountryCode = "FR";

String germanyCountryCode = "DE";

String japanCountryCode = "JP";

String mexicoCountryCode = "MX";

String ukCountryCode = "GB";

String personCountry = "US";

int personAge = 21;

if (personCountry == "US" && personAge >= 21) {

 customMessage = "cheers";

}

if (personCountry == "US" && personAge < 21) {

 customMessage = "sorry";

}

if (personCountry == "ET" && personAge >= 18) {

 customMessage = "T' chen chen";

}

if (personCountry == "ET" && personAge < 18) {

 customMessage = "Yiqirta";

}

if (personCountry == "FR" && personAge >= 18) {

 customMessage = '\u00C0' + "votre sant" + '\u00C0';

}

if (personCountry == "FR" && personAge < 18) {
```

```java
  customMessage = "Pardon";

}
if (personCountry == "DE" && personAge >= 16) {
 customMessage = "Prost";

}
if (personCountry == "DE" && personAge < 18) {
 customMessage = "Es tut uns leid";

}
if (personCountry == "JP" && personAge >= 20) {
 customMessage = "Kanpai";

}
if (personCountry == "JP" && personAge < 18) {
 customMessage = "Gomen' nasai";

}
if (personCountry == "MX" && personAge >= 18) {
 customMessage = "Salud";

}
if (personCountry == "MX" && personAge < 18) {
 customMessage = "Lo siento";

}
if (personCountry == "GB" && personAge >= 18) {
 customMessage = "Cheers";

}
if (personCountry == "GB" && personAge < 18) {
 customMessage = "Sorry";

}
if (personCountry.isEmpty() || personAge < 0 ||
```

```
personAge > 100) {

  System.out.println("Inaccurate user input");

} else {

  System.out.println(customMessage);

}
```

33. Yes, the associated while statement for a do while loop is needed. When you place the do keyword in your source code in Java, it must have an associated while loop as the compiler will look for it.

34. No, a do while loop must have an associated while loop.

35. It prints 0 nine times.

36.
```
int i = 1;

do {

        if (i == 1) {

                System.out.println("\"The number of days
                in a "

                + "common year\"");

        }

        System.out.print(i + " ");

        i++;

} while (i < 366);
```

37. There's nothing stopping the loop from terminating so it keeps on *going and going* like the energizer bunny. The way to correct this is to add an increment statement after the condition.

38. It prints 2-6. The increment is done in a separate statement before the print statement. If you were expecting the loop to print 1...5, then change the order of the while block so that the print statement is done first and then i is incremented.

39.

a) The loop iterates a total of 80 times.

b) `int count = 0;`

```
for (int i = 1; i <= 10; i++) {
    count++;
    for (int j = 1; j <= 7; j++) {
        count++;
    }
}
System.out.println("count = " + count);
```

40. The `continue` statement causes the print statement to not be reached. Remember, the `continue` keyword skips the rest of the block and forces the next iteration to start. You can correct the program by removing the continue keyword as it's not needed.

41. No, they both print 1...10.

42. The values 2...13.

43. No, loop a prints 2...13, while loop b prints 1...12. Notice that in loop a, i is incremented in a separate statement compared to loop b. To make loop a equivalent to loop b, put the increment after the print statement.

44. It prints 1...4, and then -3...11. This example is to demonstrate that the items you put inside a for loop are optional. However, it's important to write some type of condition that will stop the flow of the iteration because without it the loop will continue indefinitely.

45. It prints the following:

```
i = 1 i = 2 i = 3 i = 4 i = 5
j = 1 j = 2 j = 3 j = 4
```

46.
```
char exclamatoryMark = '\u0021';
char deleteCode = '\u007F';
while (exclamatoryMark < deleteCode) {
    System.out.print((char) exclamatoryMark + " ");
    exclamatoryMark++;
}
```

47. a)

```
int i = 1;
for (int j = 1; j <= 20; j++, i++) {
        System.out.println(i + " * " + j + " = " + i
        * j);
}
```

b)

```
int i = 1;
for (int j = 1; j <= 100; j++, i++) {
        System.out.println(i + " * " + j + " = " + i
        * j);
}
```

48.
```
for (int i = 1; i <= 5; i++) {
        for (int j = 1; j <= i; j++) {
            System.out.print(" * ");
        }
        System.out.println();
}
```

49.
```
for (int i = 5; i >= 1; i--) {
  for (int j = 1; j <= i; j++) {
    System.out.print("O");
  }
  System.out.println();
}
```

50.
```
for (int i = 1; i <= 5; i++) {
        for (int j = 1; j <= 5; j++) {
            if (i == 1 && j == 1) {
                System.out.print("J");
```

```
                    continue;
            } else if (i == 2 && j == 2) {
                System.out.print("A");
                continue;
            } else if (i == 3 && j == 3) {
                System.out.print("V");
                continue;
            } else if (i == 4 && j == 4) {
                System.out.print("A");
                continue;
            } else if (i == 5 && j == 5) {
                System.out.print("!");
                continue;
            }
            System.out.print(" * ");
        }
        System.out.println();
    }
51. for(int i = 1; i < 7; i++) {
      for (int j = 1; j <= 6; j++) {
        if (j % 2 == 1) {
          System.out.print("X");
        } else {
          System.out.print("O");
        }
      }
      System.out.println();
    }
```

```
52.  int i = 1;
     int j = 6;
     while (i <= 4) {
       i++;
       while (j > 0) {
         System.out.print("X");
         j--;
       }
       if (j == 0 & i == 2) {
         j = j + 4;
       } else if (j == 0 & i == 3) {
         j = j + 2;
       } else {
         j++;
       }
       System.out.println();
     }

53.  char dollarSign = '\u0024';
     for (int i = 1; i <= 4; i++) {
       for (int j = 1; j <= 5; j++) {
         System.out.print(dollarSign + " " + '\t');
       }
       System.out.println();
     }

54.  for(int i = 1; i <=5; i++) {
       for (int j = 1; j <= i; j++) {
         System.out.print("X");
```

```
  }
  for (int k = 4; k >= i; k--) {
   System.out.print("O");
  }
  System.out.println();
 }
```

55.
```java
char squareIcon = '\u25a0';
for (int i = 1; i <= 4; i++) {
 int x = 4;
 while (x > 2) {
  System.out.print("X" + " ");
  x--;
 }
 for (int square = 1; square <= i; square++) {
  System.out.print(squareIcon + " ");
 }
 int k = 2;
 while (k >= 1) {
  System.out.print(k + " ");
  k--;
 }
 System.out.println();
}
```

56.
```java
for(double a = 1; a < 2; a+=.15) {
 System.out.println(a);
}
```

57.
```java
int F_n_1 = 0;
```

```
   int F_n_2 = 1;

   int nextValue;

   System.out.println(0);

   for(int i = 1; i <= 13; i++) {

    nextValue = F_n_1 + F_n_2;

    System.out.println(nextValue);

    F_n_2 = F_n_1;

    F_n_1 = nextValue;

   }
```

58.
```
   int i = 1;

   int num = 1;

   while (true) {

    i *= 2;

    System.out.println(num + "/" + i);

    if (i == 1024)

     break;

   }
```

Chapter 4: Classes, Objects, and Methods, Oh My

In the previous chapters we built programs in which code was added to a single file. That's ok for teaching the basics of Java but in reality this is not preparing you for the real world. Production code for large applications can be massive; I'm talking about hundreds of thousands of lines! Can you imagine trying to understand a program that consists of 100,000 lines of code all squeezed into a single file? It's not impossible but it's the closest thing to it known to man. In this section you're going to learn the basics of **object oriented programming** (oop) with Java. This is a modular approach to building software so instead of stuffing code into a single file like sardines; you'll learn how to divide it into separate files which is more maintainable. This will require you to think differently as you will now be using objects to manipulate data in your code. You will learn how to build classes, how to create methods, and how to construct objects to manipulate data.

The real scoop about classes in java

Classes are a concept found in object oriented programming languages and are the template from which objects are constructed. The class contains members which are variables, methods, and constructors. Classes are extensible meaning you can build upon it, and re-usable meaning that it can be used by other classes. In Java SE 8 there are over 4,000 pre-built classes that developers can re-use to speed up their programming. While studying classes in the Java API is an excellent way to learn how to design your own classes, it can be quite overwhelming for someone without a solid programming foundation. Let's start with simple concepts and then build upon that.

Think about a domesticated dog. If someone asks you how to describe one how would you? Even though there are about 340 breeds of dogs there are common denominators they all share. For example, all dogs: sleep, eat, have four legs, and are mammals. We can simulate the attributes and behaviors of domesticated dogs by creating a class. An attribute is synonymous with an instance field. Fields are a type of variable, but the main distinction is that they're declared outside of any method. This allows them to be used throughout any portion of the class. Behaviors are what an object does. For example, barking can be described as a behavior of a dog. Behaviors are associated with the methods of a class which will be explained later on in this chapter.

The syntax for creating a class is listed below:

```
public class ClassName  {
// body
}
```

Classes can include the access modifier of `public` or no modifier at all. Access modifiers dictate how a class can be accessed by another class.

Let's create a public class named Dog. The syntax is listed below:

```
public class Dog {
}
```

Types of variables

The variables that we have been declaring thus far are local variables. These types of variables have a limited scope, or duration in which they can be used in a program. Local variables are declared inside methods or blocks of code and are terminated once the block ends. Examples of local variables are indicated in the code snippet below:

Figure 4.0: Demo of local variables.

```
public static void main(String[] args) {
  int x = 10;
  int y = 20;
  int z = 30;
}
```

In the above snippet x, y, and z are all examples of local variables.

Variables created outside methods are known as instance variables or fields. The reason for this is because when a copy or instance of the class is created, copies of the instance variables are stored in the object. All variables are stored in memory, but not all variables are treated equally. Local variables are stored in the stack while reference types like objects are stored in the heap--variables stored in the stack consume less memory than variables stored in the heap. The data on the stack is only alive for as long as the method is executing. The data on the heap is alive for as long as it's not discarded. When an object is no longer being used its automatically removed from the heap in a process called garbage collection. The C-programming language allows programmers to have more control over memory management. For example, the `malloc()` function allocates a certain amount of memory during the program execution while the `free()` function de-allocates the memory reserved.

The following code snippet is an example of instance variables in Java:

Figure 4.1: Demo of instance variables.

```
public class Burger {

  private int numberOfToppings = 5;

  private String meat;

  private String bunType;

  private boolean mayonnaise;

}
```

The identifiers `numberOfToppings`, `meat`, `bunType`, and `mayonnaise` are all instance variables. Remember, instance variables are declared outside methods--therefore, they can't be inside the main method as only local variables are allowed inside methods. Instance variables can be declared or initialized. However, to manipulate the values of instance variables this will be done via calls to methods or constructors.

A class variable is a variable in which there exists only a single copy. A class could have 10 instances but there will still remain just one copy of the variable. In other words, its location is fixed or static in memory. You declare a class variable by using the static keyword. For example, the following is an example of the `static` keyword being used:

Figure 4.2: Demo of static variables.

```
public class A {
```

```
static int a;

static int b;

static double c = 3.14;
}
```

In the above examples a, b, and c are all examples of static variables. If you want a value in Java to be unchangeable then you'll need to create a variable that's known as a constant. You do this by attaching the `static` and `final` modifiers to a variable. The following code snippet is an example of a constant in Java:

```
static final int PLANETS_IN_SOLAR_SYSTEM = 9;
```

By convention the names of constants should be in all caps, and if there's more than one word then you should separate each one with an underscore (_). Trying to change the value of a constant will lead to a compile error.

packages

Programmers can group related classes into packages. For example, if you have a group of classes that revolve around physic equations then you can group all of those classes into a single bundle and name the package `physics`. In theory a package is just a folder in which you place your files in. If a Java program doesn't explicitly declare a package, then all of the files in the same directly are implicitly in the same package.

Since Java is such a popular programming language there's the likelihood that software companies will use the same class name. To avoid naming collisions, Java recommends a convention for naming packages. The rules are for a company to use their domain name in reverse.

For example, my website url is: `www.purcellconsult.com`

Therefore, if I were to convert my domain name into a package using Java naming conventions the result will be: `com.purcellconsult.mypackagename`

In this example `.com` is the top-level domain, `purcellconsult` is the name of the website, and mypackagename represents the name of the package. Let's assume I decide to call the package "burger," the package name will therefore be:

```
com.purcellconsult.burger
```

Package names by convention are created in all lowercase letters.

Let's assume that inside of the burger package there's a class called `Hamburger`.

The fully qualified path name would be:

`com.purcellconsult.burger.Hamburger`

Once you have created the package structure the next step is to include the package statement at the very top of your java file. This is a way to group related classes into the package.

For example, this statement will go at the very top of the java file before the class declaration:

`package com.purcellconsult.burger;`

The next step is to compile and run the Java file. To do this you must understand file structures and know where the path or location of the java file is. Once you know this you can use the `javac` command as normal followed by the path to where the source file is located. For example, since the source code is located in the burger folder the correct code to execute via command prompt would be:

`javac com/purcellconsult/burger/Hamburger.java`

To run the file the command will be:

`java com/purcellconsult/burger/Hamburger`

If you want to compile multiple classes in a folder at once, then you can use the following command:

`javac *.java`

The Java application programming interface (API) organizes classes into packages. For example, a class which we have used several times thus far is inside the `java.lang` package. This package contains the `System` class which has a static field called `out` which is used in the method call `System.out.println()`. Packages that are in the Java api package names begin with the words `java` or `javax`.

Importing classes

To view a list of packages available in Java SE 8 you can view them here: `https://docs.oracle.com/javase/8/docs/api/`

To be able to use the premade classes in your Java programs you must use the `import` statement. For example, let's assume that we want to import the Timer class in the java api.

The syntax for importing it is:

```
import javax.management.timer.Timer;
```

To import all of the classes in a particular package use this syntax:

```
package.*;
```

For example, to import all of the classes in the java.io package you'll use the following syntax:

```
import java.io.*;
```

Access modifiers

There are four access modifiers that you can use to manage the access of a variable in a Java program. They can declare a member of a class as being `public`, `private`, `protected`, or having no modifier at all.

public: This means that a member of a class is accessible to all other classes. In other words this means that any class will be able to access the public field or method. Constructors are typically declared as public. An example of a public modifier being used on an instance variable is listed below:

```
public int a;
```

private: This means that members of a class are only accessible by that class itself. Instance fields are typically made private for security purposes. This prevents other classes from accidently modifying its value which can be very difficult to notice during debugging. An example of a `private` access modifier is listed below:

```
private int b;
```

protected: This means that members of a class can be accessed by other classes in its packages and all subclasses as well. An example of protected instance variable is listed below:

```
protected int c;
```

No modifier: If members of a class don't have any modifier at all then it's implicitly known as package-private. This means that this variable can only be accessed by other classes in the same package. An example of such variable is listed below:

```
int d;
```

The table below displays the access levels of the different modifiers:

Chart of access modifiers

Figure 4.3: Chart of access modifiers.

Modifier	Class	Package	Subclass	World
private	Y	N	N	N
public	Y	Y	Y	Y
protected	Y	Y	Y	N
no modifier	Y	Y	N	N

Objects

Objects in object oriented programming languages model entities that have a state and behavior. As mentioned previously an attribute is data value and behavior is something that the object does. The object can represent a physical entity like a motorcycle or an intangible one like temperature. To declare an object you need to create a reference variable and then use the new operator followed by a call to the constructor to initialize it.

Creating objects

Refer to the following snippet of code:

```
Book paperback;
```

In the above example the variable `paperback` is created and its type is `Book`. This is similar to declaring variables of primitive types. For example:

```
int age;
```

However, the difference is the first example is creating a reference variable while the latter is a primitive type. In more technical means, primitive types store values while reference types store addresses in memory. Therefore, simply printing the value of a reference type will reveal its address which is not what you want.

The syntax for constructing an object in Java is as follows:

```
ClassName referenceName = new ClassName();
```

Therefore, to create a book object you'll use the following syntax:

```
Book paperback = new Book();
```

What the above code does is create a new book object with the reference name of **pa-perback**. Remember that reference types in Java points to a reference in memory. They're similar to pointers in C but there are some distinctions. In Java, you can't perform arithmetic operations with reference types which are allowable in C. In addition, in Java the JVM has a dynamic memory management system and frees up memory when it's no longer being referenced by an object. In C, this can be handled by the developer which makes pointers in C more flexible than reference types in Java.

You can create multiple objects which equates to multiple instances of a class. For example, the following is valid code in Java:

```
Book scienceFiction = new Book();

Book satire = new Book();

Book drama = new Book();

Book actionAdventure = new Book();
```

Methods

A **method** is a sequence of code that's encapsulated within curly braces and given a name. They're similar to functions in the C-programming language. In Java there're four components which are required when you create a method. They're method name, access modifier, return type, a pair of parenthesis, and curly braces to wrap the statements of the body inside.

The syntax for creating a method in Java that returns a value is indicated below:

```
accessModifier returnType methodName(parameter 1,
parameter 2, … , parameter n) {

// body statements

// return statement

}
```

A method can be `public, private, protected,` or have no access modifier. A method must specify a return type while the parameters are optional. The type can be any of the primitive types, or it can be a reference type like an object or array. If a method doesn't return anything then the return type should be void meaning that the method doesn't return anything. All methods have names, and by convention if it consists of multiple words then the letter of the first word should be lowercase, and the first letter of subsequent words should be capitalized.

A method has parameters which are the variables that are included in the declaration of the method. The parameters can be of mixed type meaning that you can include any primitive or reference type within the parameters. The parameters must be delimited by commas (,). A method must have an associated opening and closing curly brace to put the body statements inside. If a method has a return type in the method declaration then it must return one within the method's body. If it doesn't specify a return type then the body simply executes the statements inside of the method body without returning anything. Let's take a look at some code to get a better idea of how this works.

A method that returns

A method will return to the code that invokes it if any of the following scenarios occurs:

- Completes all the statements in the body

- Reaches a return statement

- Throws an exception (covered in the last chapter)

So, let's assume that we're creating a mathematical application and want to sum up two numbers and then return the sum. Below is an example implementation:

Figure 4.4: A method with a return type.

```
public int addNumbers(int a, int b) {

  return a + b;

}
```

The access modifier is `public` which means that this method can be re-used within this class, package, or anywhere else. The return type is specified as an int which means that the method must also return an `int`. The name of the method is `addNumbers` which gives a hint to what the logic does. The method name is also a verb which is also a naming convention with methods. The body is just one line of code and it returns the sum of parameters a and b. We'll next convert this method to a `void` type so that we can analyze the difference between a method that returns something and a void one.

A method that's void

A void method doesn't return anything; it simply executes a block of statements. The syntax for creating a void method is listed below:

```
accessModifier void methodName(parameter 1, parameter 2,
..., parameter n) {

 // body statements

}
```

The parameters for a void method are optional.

Below is the previous method converted into a void type.

Figure 4.5: A method with a void type.

```
public void addNumbers(int a, int b) {

 int sum = a + b;

}
```

There are some differences between the two methods. This method specify void instead of a return type, and the body is different. In this example a local variable named int sum is created within the body of the method and it holds the sum of the two parameters which are int a and int b.

Calling a method

Now that we have learned the rules for creating methods how do we actually use it? The solution is that you'll need to call or invoke the method. A method call is when the method is being put into action. If the method is not being called, then it's not being executed. The standard way to call a non-static method is to construct an object of the class and then to call the method via the reference to the object. A non-static method is one in which the `static` keyword is not used in its declaration. As mentioned earlier in this chapter the static keyword means that the variable or method is shared between all instances of the class.

To put the method into action we're going to create a class named `Math` and then add our method to it as indicated in the code below:

```
public class Math {

 public int addNumbers(int a, int b) {

  return a + b;

 }

}
```

Now, in order to keep our code clean I'm going to create a separate class to create the object and test the method. This additional class will also contain a main method to serve as the entry point in the Java program. In the academic realm of teaching Java this type of class is known as a *driver class,* as it drives other classes--this term is not used often outside of the academic sphere. We will call this additional class `MathTester.java.` Once that's done, we'll create the class, create an instance of it, and then invoke the method. We'll store the method call in a variable of the same type which is `int` so that we can print the results to confirm that the method is functioning properly. This can all be seen in the following snippet of code:

Figure 4.6: Invoking a method demo.

```
public class MathTester {

  public static void main(String[] args) {

   Math sum = new Math();

   int result = sum.addNumbers(100, 300);

   System.out.println("The sum is " + result);

  }

}
```

The output is 400 which is correct.

Blow-by-blow analysis

Let's analyze `MathTester.java.` We see that the class is created followed by the main method. Inside of it an object is constructed in the following statement:

```
Math sum = new Math();
```

When this is done an instance of the class fields and methods are stored in the sum reference variable. From there, the method can be invoked or called. In order to invoke a method you use the reference variable, followed by a dot operator (.), followed by the name of the method with the arguments inside the parenthesis. The arguments of a method are the values that are being passed into a method, so in this example the arguments are `100` and `300`. Remember, the arguments must match the types of the method signature. A method signature includes the name of the method and its parameters, so in this example the method signature will be:

```
addNumbers(int, int)
```

Therefore, if a `double` was used in the arguments then a compile error would occur due to the mismatch in types.

It's perfectly fine to store the method call in an `int` type since the return type for the method is an integer. That's why the following statement is legal:

```java
int result = sum.addNumbers(100, 300);
```

Since result now contains the integer that's returned we can print result to see what the value is which is 400.

Overloading methods

Methods can be overloaded, or in other words there can be multiple methods in a class with the same name as long as their signatures are different. For example, the following is permissible in Java:

```java
public void addNumbers(int a, int b) {
        int numbers = a + b;

}
public void addNumbers(double a, double b) {
        double numbers = a + b;

}
```

The difference between the two methods is that one has parameters of type `int`, while the other has parameters of type `double`.

Constructors

Constructors are important components in Java. They initialize objects and can also manipulate the data of instance variables. In matter of fact, constructors are so important in Java that if the programmer doesn't explicitly create one, then a default no-argument constructor is supplied by the compiler. Constructors are similar to methods. Here are the differences.

- Constructors must have the same name as the class name

- Constructors may not specify a return type; not even void

- Constructors can be used to initialize objects

- Constructors aren't called explicitly like methods. They're called implicitly with the new operator

To better understand constructors lets create a class. I'm a big fan of burgers, and have probably eaten every type in existence. One of the most common types of burgers are a hamburger which is a sandwich which consists of circular cooked beef patties placed in between buns which are also circular in shape. Let's create a class that simulates the hamburger. The first thing to do is create the class which is indicated in the code snippet below:

```java
public class Burger {

}
```

The next thing we'll do is create the constructor. Remember, constructors must have the same name as the class and exclude a `return` type including `void`. The updated code snippet is listed below:

```java
public class Burger {

  public Burger() {

  }

}
```

We created a no-argument constructor inside the class, but the class doesn't do anything. The next thing to do is create some instance variables that are associated with a burger. For simplicity sakes we can define some constraints for the burger. Let's say that the burger can have up to three beef patties, lettuce, tomatoes, onion, and pickle. Let's convert these attributes into fields for the class which is listed below:

```java
public class Burger {

        int numberOfBeefPatties;

        String lettuce;

        String tomato;

        String onion;

        String pickle;

        public Burger() {

        }

}
```

Next, we're going to use the constructor to initialize the values of the instance variables. We do this by creating parameters in the constructor and then setting the instance variables equal to the parameters. The updated code is listed below:

```
public class Burger {

    int numberOfBeefPatties;

    String lettuce;

    String tomato;

    String onion;

    String pickle;


    public Burger(int beef, String let, String tom,
    String oni, String pic) {

        if (beef > 0 && beef < 4)

            numberOfBeefPatties = beef;

        lettuce = let;

        tomato = tom;

        onion = oni;

        pickle = pic;

    }

}
```

As mentioned previously the constructor initializes the state of objects, so that's what the updated code is doing. Notice that the parameter names of the constructors are different from the names of the instance variables. If the parameter names are equal to the instance variable names, then the compiler wouldn't know which one to refer to and will generate an error. There's a way around this, but for now we'll stick to this strategy. In addition, since we need to confirm that a customer can select a maximum number of three patties, a conditional should be included to ensure that the correct number is entered.

The next step is to create another class to test the code. The class we'll create will be called BurgerTester.java. The purpose is to test the values that have been initialized in the object. Below is the sample code:

```
public class BurgerTester {

    public static void main(String[] args) {

        Burger hamburger = new Burger(2, "lettuce",
        "tomato","onion", "pickle");

        System.out.println(hamburger.
        numberOfBeefPatties);

        System.out.println(hamburger.lettuce);

        System.out.println(hamburger.tomato);

        System.out.println(hamburger.onion);

        System.out.println(hamburger.pickle);

        }

    }
```

Blow-by-blow analysis

The result that's printed is:

2

lettuce

tomato

onion

pickle

When the burger object is constructed, the constructor arguments must match the type of its parameters. In this case the constructor arguments must be: int, String, String, String, String. Creating a no-argument constructor will generate an error because there's no non-argument constructor in this class. The Java compiler will only provide a default no-argument constructor if the class doesn't explicitly contain one, but since this class does then the Java compiler will use the one listed in the class by default. After entering the arguments for the constructor the next step is to print them to verify the code. However, one simply can't print the reference to the object as this will provide information about the object which is not the same as the values for the instance variables.

For example, look at the following code snippet:

```
System.out.println(hamburger);
```

When the code was printed the result was:

```
Burger@139a55
```

This is not cool. In order to access the value of an instance variable the object reference name must be used followed by the dot operator. The syntax for doing so is:

```
referenceName.memberName;
```

This is why the value of 2 was printed when the following code was executed:

```
System.out.println(hamburger.numberOfBeefPatties);
```

Default values

Instance variables in Java do not need to be explicitly initialized before they're accessed--this is different from local variables which must be initialized before they're used. If instance variables are not provided initial values then Java will implicitly supply them in your program so that your program will be in a stable state. Uninitialized data has been a common source for bugs in programming history. The default values for the data types in Java are listed in the table below:

Figure 4.7: Default values in Java table.

Data Type	Default Value
byte	0
short	0
int	0
long	0L
float	0.0f
double	0.0d
char	'u0000'
String (or other object)	null
boolean	false

The following program tests the default values for instance variables in Java.

Figure 4.8: Tests the default values in Java.

```
public class DefaultValues {
    byte a;
```

```
short b;

int c;

long d;

float e;

double f;

char g;

boolean h;

String i;

DefaultValues j;


public static void main(String[] args) {

    DefaultValues test = new DefaultValues();

    System.out.println("Default value for byte is
    " + test.a);

    System.out.println("Default value for short
    is " + test.b);

    System.out.println("Default value for int is
    " + test.c);

    System.out.println("Default value for long is
    " + test.d);

    System.out.println("Default value for float is
    " + test.e);

    System.out.println("Default value for double
    is " + test.f);

    System.out.println("Default value for char is
    " + test.g);

    System.out.println("Default value for
    boolean is " + test.h);

    System.out.println("Default value for String
    is " + test.i);
```

```
System.out.println("Default value for
DefaultValues is " + test.j);
        }
}
```

The output is the following:

```
Default value

for byte is 0

Default value

for short is 0

Default value

for int is 0

Default value

for long is 0

Default value

for float is 0.0

Default value

for double is 0.0

Default value

for char is

Default value

for boolean is false

Default value

for String is null

Default value

for DefaultValues is null
```

The char value of u0000 is null which is why nothing appears when test.g is printed.

Overloading constructors

It's possible to create multiple constructors in the same class file. Even though constructors all have the same name they're differentiated from each other by their signature. You can't have the same constructors with identical parameters as that will lead to a compile time error. For example, the following code snippet is legal in Java:

```
public class A {

    public A(int x) {

    }


    public A(int x, int y) {

    }


    public A(int x, int y, int z) {

    }

}
```

You can invoke each constructor by passing the appropriate number of arguments. An example of how to do this is indicated below:

```
A a1 = new A(5);          // invokes the first constructor

A a2 = new A(100,200);    // invokes the second constructor

A a3 = new A(1,2,3);      // invokes the third constructor
```

Constructing a no-argument constructor will lead to a compile time error since all the constructors in the program have parameters.

```
A a4 = new A(); // invalid in this example
```

This keyword

In `Burger.java` we created a constructor that had parameters that were poorly named which could make code difficult to follow. In this case the this keyword should be considered. The `this` keyword is used when you have parameter names that are identical to the names of the instance variables, and you want to tell the compiler to refer to the instance variable. Therefore, the code from `Burger.java` could be updated as follows:

Figure 4.9: This keyword example.

```java
public class Burger {

    int numberOfBeefPatties;

    String lettuce;

    String tomato;

    String onion;

    String pickle;


    public Burger(int numberOfBeefPatties, String
    lettuce, String tomato, String onion, String
    pickle) {

        if (numberOfBeefPatties > 0 &&
        numberOfBeefPatties < 4)

        this.numberOfBeefPatties =
        numberOfBeefPatties;

        this.lettuce = lettuce;

        this.tomato = tomato;

        this.onion = onion;

        this.pickle = pickle;

    }

}
```

Notice that the constructor parameters and the instance variables are identical.

Setters

A **setter method,** also known as *mutator* sets the value for a private field. By convention, the name of the method begins with the word `set`. For example, `setTemperature()`, and `setTime()` are all examples of setter method names.

Getters

A getter method, also known as an accessor retrieves the private variables of a particular class. By convention, the name of getter methods begins with `get`. For example, `getTemperature()`, and `getTime()` are examples of getter method names.

Below is a class called `Book.java` that has three instance variables which are `price`, `authorFirstName`, and `authorLastName`.

Figure 4.10: Getter and setter method demo.

```java
public class Book {

    private double price;

    private String authorFirstName;

    private String authorLastName;


    public double setPrice(double price) {

        this.price = price;

        return price;

    }

    public void getPrice() {

        System.out.println(price);

    }

    public String setAuthorFirstName(String
    authorFirstName) {

        this.authorFirstName = authorFirstName;

        return authorFirstName;

    }

    public void getAuthorFirstName() {

        System.out.println(authorFirstName);

    }
```

```
public String setAuthorLastName(String
authorLastName) {

    this.authorLastName = authorLastName;

    return authorLastName;

}
public void getAuthorLastName() {

    System.out.println(authorLastName);

}
}
```

Below is the driver class that tests the methods. The class is called `BookTester.java` and is written below:

```
public class BookTester {

    public static void main(String[] args) {

        Book bookOne = new Book();

        bookOne.setAuthorFirstName("Doug");

        bookOne.getAuthorFirstName();

        bookOne.setAuthorLastName("Purcell");

        bookOne.getAuthorLastName();

    }
}
```

The values printed are:

```
24.95
```

```
Doug
```

```
Purcell
```

Why use setters and getters?

There are many reasons why a developer can use setter and getter methods instead of just exposing the inward fields of a class.

Encapsulation: When the instance fields of a class are `private` and the methods that manipulate/retrieve them are public, then encapsulation is achieved because the data is hidden from outside classes. Therefore, its data is prevented from being manipulated from outside classes.

Reduces complexity: Using setter and getter methods could make a program simpler by ensuring that just the relevant details of an object are exposed.

Easy to extend: If other functionality needs to be added later to instance variables then only the getter and setter methods needs to be updated.

Static fields

Static fields are associated with the class rather than the object. A class can have many instances but there will only remain one copy of a static field or class variable. Static fields can invoke a method alone without the use of objects since they belong to a class. Look at the following code snippet which shows static variables being printed:

Figure 4.11: Static field demo.

```
public class Static {

    private static int ten = 10;

    private static String greeting = "Hello";

    private static char zee = 'Z';

    private static boolean truth = true;


    public static void main(String[] args) {

        System.out.println(ten);

        System.out.println(greeting);

        System.out.println(zee);

        System.out.println(truth);

    }

}
```

Static variables must be declared outside of a method. If they're declared inside of a method then a compile error will generate. Below is an example of a static method:

Figure 4.12: Static method demo.

```
public class StaticShock {

    public static void charge() {

        System.out.println("Static Shock!");

    }


    public static void main(String[] args) {

        StaticShock.charge();

    }

}
```

The output will be: `Static Shock!`

To invoke a static method use the following format: `ClassName.methodName();`

Remember, since static fields belong to the class an object doesn't need to be made to invoke them.

enums

An enum is a special type that allows a variable to be a set of predefined constants. A constant in Java is one in which the value is immutable, so it's implicitly `static` and `final`. Enums in Java are very powerful, as they're actually a type of class and can include instance variables and fields. Some examples of `enums` are days of the week, months in year, cities in a country, and cardinal directions.

Creating enums

An enum in Java is declared with the enum keyword. The syntax for creating enums is listed below:

```
optionalModifier enum EnumName {

  // statements

}
```

Like classes, enums can only be public or contain no-access modifiers. Below is an example of an enum:

Figure 4.13: Enum demo.

```
public enum CitrusFruit {

    LEMONS, GRAPE_FRUIT, ORANGES, TANGERINES, LIMES,
    POMELO, BLOOD_ORANGE, BUDDHAS_HAND;

    public static void main(String[] args) {

        CitrusFruit fruit = CitrusFruit.LEMONS;

        System.out.println(fruit);

    }

}
```

The following is what's printed:

LEMONS

Iterating over enums

One way to iterate over enums is to use the `foreach` loop which was introduced in Java 5. This is a modified version of the `for` loop which allows you to iterate over elements of an array, Collection, or enum. Below is the syntax on how to use the `foreach` loop for enums:

```
for (EnumName: variableName: EnumName.values()) {

  System.out.println(variableName);

}
```

The `values()` method allows you to get the elements of the enum. The values are then stored inside `variableName`. Once `variableName` is passed into the print method the elements of the enum will be printed. Therefore, to print all of the elements in enum `CitrusFruit` the following code will be executed:

Figure 4.14: Iterating over and printing enums demo.

```
public enum CitrusFruitTest {

    LEMONS, GRAPE_FRUIT, ORANGES, TANGERINES, LIMES,
    POMELO, BLOOD_ORANGE, BUDDHAS_HAND;

    public static void main(String[] args) {

        for (CitrusFruitTest fruit : CitrusFruitTest.
```

```
        values()) {

                System.out.println(fruit);

        }

    }

}
```

The following will be printed:

LEMONS

GRAPE_FRUIT

ORANGES

TANGERINES

LIMES

POMELO

BLOOD_ORANGE

BUDDHAS_HAND

enums with switch statements

Enums combines nicely with switch statements which were discussed in Chapter 3. Below is an example implementation:

```
public enum CitrusFruit {

            LEMONS, GRAPE_FRUIT, ORANGES, TANGERINES,

            LIMES, POMELO, BLOOD_ORANGE, BUDDHAS_HAND;

    }
```

Following is the tester class:

Figure 4.15: Enums with switch statement.

```
public class CitrusFruitTwoTester {

    CitrusFruit fruit;
```

```java
public CitrusFruitTwoTester(CitrusFruit fruit) {

    this.fruit = fruit;

}


public void getFruit() {

    switch (fruit) {

    case LEMONS:

        System.out.println(CitrusFruit.LEMONS);

        break;

    case GRAPE_FRUIT:

        System.out.println(CitrusFruit.GRAPE_
        FRUIT);

        break;

    case ORANGES:

        System.out.println(CitrusFruit.
        ORANGES);

        break;

    case TANGERINES:

        System.out.println(CitrusFruit.
        TANGERINES);

        break;

    case LIMES:

        System.out.println(CitrusFruit.LIMES);

        break;

    case POMELO:

        System.out.println(CitrusFruit.POMELO);

        break;

    case BLOOD_ORANGE:
```

```
        System.out.println(CitrusFruit.BLOOD_
        ORANGE);

        break;

    case BUDDHAS_HAND:

        System.out.println(CitrusFruit.BUDDHAS_
        HAND);

        break;

    default:

        System.out.println("Incorrect
        options!");

        break;

    }

}


public static void main(String[] args) {

    CitrusFruitTwoTester citrusOne = new
    CitrusFruitTwoTester(CitrusFruit.LEMONS);

    citrusOne.getFruit();

    CitrusFruitTwoTester citrusTwo = new
    CitrusFruitTwoTester(CitrusFruit.GRAPE_
    FRUIT);

    citrusTwo.getFruit();


    CitrusFruitTwoTester citrusThree = new
    CitrusFruitTwoTester(CitrusFruit.ORANGES);

    citrusThree.getFruit();


    CitrusFruitTwoTester citrusFour = new
    CitrusFruitTwoTester(CitrusFruit.
    TANGERINES);
```

```
        citrusFour.getFruit();

        CitrusFruitTwoTester citrusFive = new
        CitrusFruitTwoTester(CitrusFruit.LIMES);

        citrusFive.getFruit();

    }

}
```

The following is printed:

LEMONS

GRAPE_FRUIT

ORANGES

TANGERINES

LIMES

Blow-by-blow analysis

The file enum CitrusFruit creates the enum with its constants. CitrusFruitTwoTester is the driver class which tests the enum. It declares an instance variable called fruit which is of type CitrusFruit. It then creates a constructor that takes in an argument of CitrusFruitTwoTester, and then set it equal to fruit. A void method is created, and inside of it is a switch statement that prints different citrus fruits depending on the case.

Chapter 4 Re-factored

In this chapter you got a basic overview of some of the concepts that make Java object oriented. We took a look at classes, objects, packages, access modifiers, methods, and constructors just to name a few. Some of the advantages of object oriented programming are increased software productivity, improved maintainability, code re-use, and data encapsulation. However, very few things in life are immune to drawbacks. There are some issues with oop such as being unnatural to learn for those who are not familiar with oop languages and typically larger codebases than programs written in a procedural language. If you need more practice with oop then re-read this chapter, go through the questions, break some code, and have some fun.

Chapter 4 Exercises

1. T or F: Local variables don't need to be initialized before used.

2. T or F: Instance variables don't need to be initialized before used.

3. T or F: A class's private fields can be manipulated by its methods.

4. T or F: You can call another method from within a method.

5. T or F: Instance variables can be used inside methods.

6. T or F: Instance variables can be declared anywhere outside of the class's methods.

7. T or F: A constructor creates an object.

8. T or F: A parameter is an example of an instance variable.

9. T or F: One way of initializing instance variables is by setting the values of an object when calling its constructor.

10. T or F: Primitive types cannot be used to call objects.

11. T or F: An object can store primitive values.

12. T or F: You can tell from a variable's declared type if it's a primitive or reference type.

13. T or F: An object is an instance of a class, while a class is a special type of object.

14. T or F: A class is synonymous with an object.

15. T or F: If a method is never called then it's never used.

16. T or F: In order to call a method an object must be constructed.

17. T or F: A constructor is equal to a method.

18. T or F: Local variables are stored in the heap in memory.

19. T or F: Instance variables are stored in the stack in memory.

20. T or F: A default constructor is supplied for every class that doesn't explicitly define one.

21. T or F: To create an object in memory you must use the new keyword.

22. T or F: If a class has no default constructor, and the instance variables are not hardcoded into the program, then the values of instance variables are set to their default values.

23. T or F: An instance variable is stored in the heap of objects.

24. T or F: If you want to perform a task in a program then it can be written inside a method.

25. T or F: A method must return something.

26. T or F: An object can be used to create an instance of a class.

27. T or F: Each method must specify a parameter.

28. T or F: To call a method of an object you need to use the dot operator (.)

29. T or F: The parameters of a method can be of mixed type. For example, you can have int, byte, char, float, and double as parameters.

30. T or F: A method only needs to have an identifier. Its type is not needed, nor are statements inside its body.

31. T or F: The arguments in a method must match the type in the parameter list.

32. T or F: The attributes of a class are its data.

33. T or F: You can declare a variable private, protected, or public inside a method.

34. T or F: The name of a constructor may be different than the name of the class.

35. T or F: There can only be one class per java file.

36. T or F: If the class is defined inside a package, then the package statement should be the first statement.

37. T or F: If a package statement is not explicitly included in a source file, then all of the Java files in the same folder are implicitly implied as being in the same package.

38. T or F: Import statements can be written anywhere in the program.

39. T or F: A class can be made public or it can exclude any access modifiers.

40. T or F: If you create a constructor which initializes an instance variable, then this instance variable can't be overridden.

41. T or F: If you create a constructor then this will override the default one.

42. T or F: The following syntax is legal:

```
public void methodOne() {

 methodTwo();
```

}

43. T or F: There's no difference between the following snippets of code:

    a) `Object obj;`

    b) `Object obj = new Object();`

44.

    a) Create an enum named DogType that contains the following constants: PIT_BULL, DALAMTION, TERRIER, BOXER.

    b) Iterate over the enum and print all of the values of it.

45. Inside a package named method there are three more packages named: `one`, `two`, and `three`. Inside package one are two files which are: `A.java` and `Main.java`. In folder two there's a java file named `B.java`. Inside folder three there's a java file named `C.java`. `Main.java` contains the main method. Observe `Main.java` and determine **which statements** create errors when compiled, and which ones don't.

Here's the code of `A`, `B`, `C`, and `Main.java` respectively.

```java
package method.one;

public class A {

    public void one() {

        System.out.println(":)");

    }
    public void two() {

        System.out.println(":(");

    }
    public void three() {

        System.out.println(":0");

    }

}
```

```
-- -- -- -- --
package method.two;
public class B {
    public void dog() {
        System.out.println("woof woof!");
    }
    private void cat() {
        System.out.println("meow!");
    }
    protected void cow() {
        System.out.println("moow!");
    }
}
-- -- -- -- --
package method.three;
public class C {
    public int a;
    private double b;
    protected String c;
}
-- -- -- -- --
package method.one;
import method.two.B;
import method.three.C;
public class Main {
    public static void main(String[] args) {
        A a = new A();
```

```
        a.one();

        a.two();

        a.three();

        B b = new B();

        b.dog();

        b.cat();

        b.cow();

        C c = new C();

        System.out.println(c.a);

        System.out.println(c.b);

        System.out.println(c.c);

    }

}
```

Chapter 4 Exercises Answers

1. False. Unlike instance variables or variables declared outside classes, local variables need to be initialized before used.

2. True. Instance variables can be used before they're initialized. To prevent errors from happening Java provides default values to instance variables.

3. True. The type of method that manipulates a field is a setter; the type of method that accesses a field is a getter.

4. True. This is legal in Java.

5. True. Instance variables or local variables can be used inside methods.

6. True. Variables created inside methods are local methods and scope is limited to the end of the block in which it was created.

7. False. The new keyword creates a new object in memory. The constructor initializes the state of the object.

8. False: A parameter is an example of a local variable.

9. True. If a constructor has parameters then arguments could be passed to it when invoked. These arguments can then initialize the respective instance variables.

10. True. Only a reference type can call an object.

11. True. Primitives stored in objects are stored in the heap in memory. Primitives not stored inside an object are stored on the stack.

12. True. There are eight primitive types in Java which are: byte, `short`, `integer`, `long`, `char`, `float`, `double`, and `boolean`. Everything else is a reference type.

13. False. While an object is an instance of a class, a class is not a special type of object.

14. False. Objects are instances of classes, but they're not equal to classes.

15. True. A method can only be executed if it's called.

16. False. If a method is `static` then it can be called from the class in which it was created. The syntax for calling it is: `ClassName.methodName();`

17. False. In the Java programming language they're similar but not equal.

18. False. They're stored in the stack.

19. False. They're stored in the heap since they're a part of an object.

20. True. It's supplied by the compiler when it's not written in the class, but it's overridden if the class defines one.

21. True. Simply declaring reference variables doesn't create an object as the new operator is what creates it in memory.

22. True. Instance variables may be explicitly defined in the program even though it's not common. They can also be initialized via a call to the constructor.

23. True. An instance variable is stored in the heap of an object while local variables are stored in the stack.

24. True. Methods allow programmers to modularize a program by separating its tasks.

25. False. A method can return something if it specifies a return type or it can simply execute statements and return nothing in which case it will be specified as `void`.

26. True. When an object is created it holds copies of the members of a class.

27. False. A method has the option to specify a parameter but it doesn't have to.

28. True. The dot operator allows programmers to access members of a class, and methods are members of a class.

29. True. Parameters have no restrictions of the types that can be used.

30. True. Although a bare bones method with no statements is not very helpful. For example, the following is legal in Java:

```
void a( ) {

}
```

31. True. If the arguments of a method call don't match its parameters then a compile error will occur.

32. True. Attributes is synonymous with fields.

33. False. You can only do this for instance variables, or those declared outside of a method.

34. False. The name of the constructor must equal the name of the class.

35. False. There can be multiple of classes inside each Java file, but there can only be one public class name.

36. True. It should be at the top of the source file and there can only be one package statement per source file.

37. True. All source files in the same folder are automatically assumed to be part of the same package.

38. False. They must be written between package statements and the class declaration.

39. True. The main class of a java program can be `public` or exclude an access modifier.

40. False. It can be overridden through the use of a method.

41. True. Java supplies a default constructor or less one is declared inside a class.

42. True. This is legal syntax in Java.

43. False, in snippet a, a reference is created, and in snippet b a new object is created in which the reference points to.

44.

a)

```
public enum DogType {
```

```
        PIT_BULL, DALAMTION, TERRIER, BOXER
}
```

b)

```
public class DogTypeTest {
        public static void main(String[] args) {
                for (DogType i : DogType.values()) {
                        System.out.println(i);
                }
        }
}
```

45. The following statements are legal:

```
    A a = new A();
    a.one();
    a.two();
    a.three();
    B b = new B();
    b.dog();
    C c = new C();
    System.out.println(c.a);
```

The following statements are illegal:

```
b.cat();
b.cow();
System.out.println(c.b);
System.out.println(c.c);
```

The reason why the statements are illegal is that private and protected members have more restrictions. A public class member can be seen anywhere, but this is not the case with `private` or `protected` variables. Private members can only be seen from the class itself while protected members can be seen by current class, subclasses, or any class in the same package. Since `Main.java` is located outside of the package, a compile error will occur when trying to access a protected or private member.

Chapter 5: Inheritance, Polymorphism, and Interfaces

In chapter four we were introduced to basic object oriented topics and in this chapter we're going to build upon that. We're going to learn about inheritance, interfaces, abstract classes, polymorphism, and a bunch of other topics with quirky names. These topics may look intimidating, but it's more bark than bite. Mastering the concepts in this chapter will equip developers with some of the most powerful features in Java.

Inheritance

Imagine that you wrote a program for a client that contains 10 classes. For simplicity sakes we'll say that the classes are named class A-J. Therefore, the first class is `class A`, the second class is `class B`, and so forth. All of the classes have their own separate methods. Now, let's imagine that a week later your client updates their requirements and you now realize that classes B-J will all require all the a five methods that are found in `class A.` How would you include those methods in the other classes? Well, one strategy is that you could literally copy and paste the methods in `class A` to those of the other classes. This will work but the program will become more bloated as it will contain redundant code. The more elegant solution is to use what's known as inheritance which is when a class derives the features of another class. The class that's being derived from is called the super class, and the class that's doing the deriving is called the subclass. One way to think of this is with the parent child relationship. For example, the parent is can be associated with the super class as the child or the subclass inherits attributes from the parent, just like how a child would inherits genes from their parents.

The syntax for inheriting the fields and attributes of a class is listed below:

```
accessModifier ClassName extends SuperClass {

 // statements

}


public class A {

}


public class B extends A {

}
```

In the above example class A is the super class or parent and class B is the subclass or child since it extends class A. With inheritance there are a couple of things to keep in mind.

The rules of inheritance

Private instance fields or methods can't be inherited: The private access-modifier only allows the current class to access its members. Therefore, when a subclass inherits from a super class access-modifiers play a key and private members of a class are not inherited.

Inheritance creates an *is-a* relationship: An instance of a subclass is also considered an instance of the parent class. One way to remember this is to think of this in terms of descendants. For example, imagine that at a family dinner there's a grandmother, daughter, and grandson. The daughter *is a* descendant of the grandmother and the grandson *is a* descendant of the grandmother as well. This is one way to think of an *is-a* relationship.

Super classes are normal Java classes: A super class may have the common ingredients found in a typical Java file such as constructors, fields, and methods with bodies.

A subclass may be different than a superclass: A subclass inherits the fields and methods of the superclass but it can override or change the methods. However, the signature for the overridden method must be identical to that of the original or less a compile error will occur.

Subclass can access overridden methods: A subclass can create new methods, and it can also access the methods in the super class by using the super keyword.

A subclass can access super class constructor: As again, this must be done with the super keyword which calls the superclass constructor.

An example of inheritance

The following code contains a superclass named A.java:

Figure 5.0: Super class example.

```java
public class A {

    private int a;

    protected int b;

    public int c;

    int d;


    public A() {

        System.out.println("This is class A
        constructor");

    }
    public A(int b, int c) {

        this.b = b;

        this.c = c;

        System.out.println(b + c);

    }
    public A(int b, int c, int d) {

        this.b = b;

        this.c = c;

        this.d = d;

        System.out.println(b * c * d);

    }
```

```java
public void foo() {

    System.out.println("foo");

}
public void bar() {

    System.out.println("bar");

}
public void foobar() {

    System.out.println("foobar");

}
public void foofoo() {

    System.out.println("foofoo");

}
public void abc() {

    System.out.println("abc");

}

}
```

The class contains four fields of varying access levels, three constructors, and five simple methods that just print something. The following is a subclass of class A called class B which is listed below:

Figure 5.1: Inheritance example.

```java
public class B extends A {

}
```

As you can see, class B extends class A but is literally empty. Now, let's create another class to see what class B inherits from class A. The class is called InheritanceTester and is listed below:

Figure 5.2: Inheritance test example.

```java
public class InheritanceTester {

    public static void main(String[] args) {
```

```
        B b = new B();

        b.foo();

        b.foobar();

    }

}
```

The output is the following:

This is class A constructor

foo

foobar

Blow-by-blow analysis

What happens when class B extends class A is that it inherits the inheritable properties of class A. Class A contains four instance fields. However, since one of them is private then that field won't be inherited by class B. Therefore, the following snippet of code will produce an error in `InheritanceTester`:

```
System.out.println(b.a);
```

Remember, `int a` found in class A is private which means that it's not inheritable. However, the `protected, public,` and package-private fields can be inherited and therefore accessed by the object. Therefore, the following statements are legal:

```
System.out.println(b.b);
```

```
System.out.println(b.c);
```

```
System.out.println(b.d);
```

Since class A contains five public methods all of them are inheritable by the subclass. Therefore, when class B extends class A it can access all of its methods. In `InheritanceTester`, an instance of class B is created and then it's used to call `foo()` and `foobar()` methods.

Method overriding

Methods from the super class can be overridden by the subclass. This is done by changing the body of the method and keeping the signature the same. For example, we're going to modify the `foo()` method found in `A.java` in class B.

Figure 5.3: Overridden method example.

```
public class BOveride extends A {

    public void foo() {

        System.out.println("This method overrides its
        super class method");

        System.out.println("foo");

    }

}
```

This method overrides the `foo()` method found in class A because while the signature is identical, the body is different. If an instance of class B is created and then `foo()` is called, then the contents of the updated method will be printed. The super class's method can be accessed inside of the subclass's method by using the `super` keyword as indicated in the code snippet below:

Figure 5.4: Super keyword example.

```
public void foo() {

  super.foo();

  System.out.println("This  method  overrides  its  super
  class method");

  System.out.println("foo");

}
```

The call to super must be the first statement or less a compile error will occur.

@Override annotation

Java provides a suite of annotations that a developer can add to their source file. In laymen terms annotations are syntax that a programmer can add to their code in order to provide compile time checks. Annotations are typically auto suggested with IDEs like Eclipse. Developers can create their own annotations, use the ones that are included by default, or import additional ones from the Java api. Annotations are kind of like a compile time contract. The developer agrees to implement something in their code or less a flag will be offset during compilation. Classes, methods, packages, and variables may be annotated. The first annotation I'm going to introduce is the @Override one. This should be used when you override a method in a subclass. This is useful because other programmers that look at your code will know when a super method is overridden in a subclass.

To use the @Override annotation simply put it before the method that's being overridden. The syntax for it is listed below:

```
@Override

public void foo() {

System.out.println("This method overrides its super class method");

System.out.println("foo");

}
```

An example translated into Java code is listed below:

Figure 5.5: Annotation example.

```
@Override

public void foo() {

  System.out.println("This method overrides its super class method");

  System.out.println("foo");

}
```

Note, the super class's method must exist or less a compile error will occur. In addition, if the signatures of the methods are not identical then that will also cause a compile error.

Annotation processing became a part of the javac compiler as of version 1.6.

Super keyword

Class A contains three constructors which are not all inherited by the subclass. However, constructors along with other super class members can be accessed via the super keyword. For example, B.java has been updated to reflect the following:

Figure 5.6: Super keyword being used.

```
public class B extends A {

        public B() {
```

```
      super(5, 10, 2);

   }

}
```

When an instance of class B is created 100 is printed. Why?

Remember, in class A we defined three constructors. When the `super` keyword is used in class B's constructor, it specified three arguments which are 5, 10, and 2. This tells the compiler to invoke the constructor in class A with the three parameters which states the following:

```
public A(int b, int c, int d) {
 this.b = b;
 this.c = c;
 this.d = d;
 System.out.println(b * c * d);
}
```

The constructor multiples the values passed into the parameter which is why 100 was printed.

Let's assume that class B was modified so that it stated the following:

```
public B() {
 super(5, 10);

 }
```

What's printed when an instance of class B is created? The answer is 15.

This keyword

In the previous chapter you learned about the `this` keyword to refer to an instance of a class. However, you can use this within a constructor to call another constructor within the same class. The format for doing so is listed below:

```
   accessModifier ConstructorName() {

    this(parameter 1, parameter 2, ...parameter n)

    // statements

   }
```

The constructor in class A has been updated to state the following:

```java
public class A {
    private int a;

    protected int b;

    public int c;

    int d;


    public A() {
        this(5, 5, 5);
        System.out.println("This is class A
        constructor");
    }


    public A(int b, int c) {
        this();
        this.b = b;
        this.c = c;
        System.out.println(b + c);
    }


    public A(int b, int c, int d) {
        this.b = b;
        this.c = c;
        this.d = d;
        System.out.println(b * c * d);
    }
}
```

`InheritanceTester.java` has been updated to state the following:

```
public class InheritanceTester {

    public static void main(String[] args) {

        A a = new A(5, 5);

    }

}
```

The following is outputted:

125

This is class A constructor

10

The `this` statement must be the first one inside the constructor or less a compile error will occur.

Blow-by-blow analysis

When the program is ran two arguments are passed into the constructor which is 5 and 5. This invokes the two parameter constructor in `class A` which contains `this()` as the first statement. This calls the no-argument constructor which also contains `this(5,5,5)` as the first statement. This statement passes those arguments into the 3-parameter constructor which then multiples the integers and print them out which is 125. It also has another print statement which is "This is class A constructor." However, the two-argument constructor hasn't finished executing its remaining statements so the remaining statements are then executed which prints the sum of the two arguments which is 10.

Polymorphism

Poly is derived from the Greek word πολύς which translates to "many" in English. Polymorphism in biology is a term that describes when something has the capability of taking on multiple forms. For example, the Scarlet tiger moth near Oxford England has three different phenotypes. Polymorphism in Java allows objects to take on many different forms. A common scenario in which polymorphism is used is when a parent class is used as reference type for a child object. Let's work through an example as it's difficult to gain a grasp of polymorphism without analyzing some code. The superclass `Cars.java` is listed below:

Figure 5.7: Polymorphism superclass example: Car.java.

```java
public class Car {

        private int speed;


        public Car(int currentSpeed) {
            speed = currentSpeed;
            System.out.println("start car...");
        }
        public void changeSpeed(int speed) {
            this.speed = speed;
        }
        public void getSpeed() {
            System.out.println(speed);
        }
        public void stopCar() {
            System.out.println("car is
            stopping...");
            this.speed = 0;
        }
        public int maxSpeed(int maxSpeed) {
            return maxSpeed;
        }
        public void hitBrakes(int deccelerate) {
            speed -= deccelerate;
            String message = (speed < 0) ? "Speed
            can't be negative" : "Your speed is now
            " + speed;
            System.out.println(message);
        }
    }
```

This super class contains one instance field, one constructor, and five public instance methods. The class outlines a simple blueprint for a generic car. There's a one-parameter constructor which accepts an integer argument and that's used as the initial speed for the car. The remaining methods manipulate the speed of the car.

`FerrariF430.java` which is Car's subclass is listed below:

Figure 5.8: Polymorphism subclass example.

```
public class FerrariF430 extends Car {

    public FerrariF430(int speed) {

        super(speed);

    }

    public void engineType() {

        System.out.println("4.3L V8");

    }

    public void steeringWheel() {

        System.out.println("manettino steering
        wheel-mounted control knob");

    }

}
```

This class has one constructor and two public instance methods. The constructor accepts one argument of type int, and the body of it has a single statement which contains a call to the super() method with the parameter as its argument. The statements in the constructor of the super class are executed. The subclass also contains two additional methods which just print out information about `FerrariF430`.

In `CarTest.java` several instances of the class are created as indicated below:

```
public class CarTest {

    public static void main(String[] args) {

        Car sedan = new Car(50);

        FerrariF430 ferrari = new FerrariF430(100);

        FerrariF430 spider = new FerrariF430();
```

```
            FerrariF430 f430 = new Car(196);

    }

}
```

However, there are some issues with the following instances. Can you detect them?

The first two instances are fine. However, the last two will generate compile errors. Look at the following code snippet:

```
FerrariF430 spider = new FerrariF430();
```

The `FerrariF430` class constructor has a parameter of type `int`, but the constructor in this statement is empty which generates the compile error. To correct the error pass an integer argument to the constructor.

Look at the following snippet of code:

```
FerrariF430 f430 = new Car(196);
```

The reason why this generates a compile error is because `Car` cannot be converted to type `FerrariF430`. When you try and do this you're trying to convert a super class into a subclass which is not permissible. Remember, inheritance specifies an `is-a` relationship. A subclass is a type of super class, but a super class is not necessarily a type of subclass. The reason being is that the subclass could differ from that of its super class with overridden methods or additional ones.

For example, you could try and get by this by casting Car to FerrariF430 like listed below:

```
FerrariF430 f430 = (FerrariF430)new Car(196);
```

This will compile without errors, but when you run it you'll see an error that states: Exception in thread "main" java.lang.ClassCastException: Car cannot be cast to FerrariF430 at CarTest.main(CarTest.java:9)

The text in "Exception in thread "main" java.lang.ClassCastException: Car cannot be cast to FerrariF430 at CarTest.main(CarTest.java:9)" should be different font type.

With Java you can only cast between the same type of objects. Since Car is not the same type as FerrarirF430 then a runtime error occurs. However, you can take advantage of the polymorphic features in Java by writing this statement instead:

```
Car f430 = new FerrariF430(196);
```

The reason why you can do this is because `FerrariF430` extends the `Car`, therefore the super class can be used as a reference type when invoking a `FerrariF430` object. This is a common way that polymorphism is implemented in Java. In chapter 8 we'll explore Collections which contains multiple examples of polymorphism.

If you want to cast an object from one type to the next then the types must be compatible. For example, the following statement is legal:

```
Car superCar = (Car)new FerrariF430(0);
```

Here's the updated `CarTest` class which is listed below:

```
public class CarTest {

    public static void main(String[] args) {

        Car sedan = new Car(50);

        sedan.getSpeed();

        sedan.hitBrakes(10);

        sedan.getSpeed();

        Car ferrari = new FerrariF430(100);

        ferrari.getSpeed();

        ferrari.changeSpeed(100);

        ferrari.getSpeed();

        ferrari.stopCar();

        ferrari.getSpeed();

        ferrari.hitBrakes(0);

        FerrariF430 spider = new FerrariF430(0);

        spider.engineType();

        spider.steeringWheel();

    }

}
```

The output is the following:

starting car...

50

Your speed is now 40

40

starting car...

100

100

car is stopping...

0

Your speed is now 0

starting car...

4.3L V8

manettino steering wheel-mounted control knob

Interfaces

According to dictionary.com an interface can be defined as a common boundary of two bodies, spaces, or phases. This definition is useful for understanding interfaces in Java. An interface can be described as a reference type similar to a class with the exception that it contains solely the behaviors or methods. Interfaces are a key component in OOP and it's used often in the Java API. The reason for this is that interfaces enable **abstraction**, or the hiding of certain implementation details from the end-user while exposing only the essential details of the object. Therefore, the end-user doesn't need to know the technical specifics of a method; they simply need to know what it does and how to invoke it.

The end-user will have a high-level overview as opposed to a low-level one. They'll be looking from the outside of the object as opposed to the inside. For example, the `System.out.println()` method was used countless of times throughout this book in order to print output. We're not concerned that all of the characters printed by a PrintStream are converted into bytes using the platform's default encoding; we just want to use it to print text.

How to declare an interface

To declare an interface you simply use the interface keyword. The syntax for doing so is listed below:

```
public interface InterfaceName {

    // body

}
```

An interface can be public or it can contain no access modifier and be assumed package-private. Therefore, the following syntax is also legal:

```
interface InterfaceName {

    // body

}
```

Like classes an interface name must be identical to its filename and include the `.java` extension. There are also a couple of things to keep in mind. Interfaces are a scheme for describing what the class does. Since classes are typically named nouns, and an adjective modifies a noun, some are in favor with naming interfaces as adjectives. If you were to look at some of the interfaces available in the Java API you'll see some interface names with the suffix *able* such as `Adjustable` or `ItemSelectable`. However, this is not standardization because an adjective doesn't make sense in every situation. Another philosophy is that since an interface is similar to a class it should be named a noun. My philosophy is to brainstorm and discover the common behaviors between classes and entities and let a meaningful name emerge out of the process. For example, if you create classes called `Rain,` `Snow,` `Sunshine,` and Cloudy, then an interface named `Weather` makes sense in this context.

The rules of interfaces

As mentioned previously, interfaces are similar to classes but they're not identical. For example, they differ on what can go inside of them, and they offer differ on how they're instantiated. Below are the rules for what's allowed for interfaces:

Abstract methods: All methods declared inside an interface are both `public` and `abstract` by default, so no additional keywords are needed. An abstract method is one that's declared but has no implementation. Abstract methods have no braces and are terminated by a semicolon. An example of an abstract method declared inside an interface is listed below:

```
void String getName(String name);
```

Constants: An interface may have constants which are variables declared with the `static` and `final` keywords. Remember, constants may not be modified or less a compile error will occur. Constants declared inside interfaces are assumed to be constants so the `static` and `final` keywords are not needed. An example of a constant declared inside an interface is listed below:

```
double eulersNumber = 2.7182818284590452353602874713527;
```

An example of a variable that's not allowed in interfaces is listed as follows: `double` x;

Interfaces cannot be instantiated: Therefore, trying to create an object of the same type as the Interface is not permitted. The following snippet of code will create a compile error:

```
interface InterfaceExample {

    public static void main(String[] args) {

        InterfaceExample test = new InterfaceExample();

    }

}
```

Interfaces cannot contain constructors: An interface may only contain constants or methods. Nothing else is permitted.

Interfaces can contain nothing: The following code is legal:

```
interface InterfaceExample {

}
```

As you can see the above example has no fields and methods and is known as a marker interface. There are several examples of **marker interfaces** in the Java API which are `Serializable, Clonnable,` and `Remote`. The purpose of a marker interface is to convey some special treatment to the implementing class. Markers in Java are a design decision and are similar to annotations.

An interface cannot be extended: To extend an interface do not use the extends keyword. Instead, use the implements keyword.

For excellent ways to learn how to design better interfaces carefully study the interfaces available in the classes in the Java API. You'll get to see oop insights from some of the world's best java programmers. Also, if you're having troubles grasping the point of interfaces then think of it this way. An interface can be described as a contract between the classes that implements it. For example, a class that uses an interface must agree to implement the methods in it.

Why the heck would you use interfaces?

Common set of methods and constants: The classes can share a common set of methods and constants without requiring them to be implemented by a common super class. Therefore, each class that implements the interface can have their own unique implementation of the method in the interface.

Provides a simple way to use a class: Interfaces create simplicity. When viewing our favorite shows we use a remote control which allows us to change channels, adjust volume, or record something. The details of how to do this are hidden from the user, but if we want to learn all of the features of a remote control we could read the user manual. A similar concept applies to interfaces. They remove the technical implementation of the class while exposing minimal details of the object.

Multiple inheritance: A program can inherit the attributes and behaviors of another class through the use of the extends keyword. The shortcoming with this is that a subclass can't inherit multiple of classes, they can only inherit from a single class. However, a workaround to this is to use interfaces as multiple of them can be implemented.

Not affected by changes to other classes: Since interfaces are made independent of other classes, it's unaffected by the changes that the classes that implement it make. Therefore, the classes that implement the interface can make changes to the underpinning code without breaking anything.

Polymorphism: Interfaces can be more advantageous than having multiple methods in a class not implementing an interface because the class can be used anywhere an interface is expected. To understand this better let's look at the following pieces of code:

Figure 5.9: Interface example.

```
public interface Remote {

    boolean turnOn();

    boolean turnOff();

    public static void main(String[] args) {
        Remote screen1 = new Screen1();
        System.out.println(screen1.turnOn());
```

```
            Remote screen2 = new Screen2();
    }


    class Screen1 implements Remote {


        public boolean turnOn() {
            return true;
        }
        public boolean turnOff() {
            return false;
        }
    }


    class Screen2 implements Remote {


        public boolean turnOn() {
            return true;
        }


        public boolean turnOff() {
            return false;
        }


    }
}
```

Blow-by-blow analysis

The interface Remote defines two methods which are `Boolean turnOn()` and `boolean turnOff()`. It also has a main method for invoking the program. The program has two classes which are `Screen1` and `Screen2`. `Screen1` implements the interface and therefore implements its methods, while `Screen2` is a normal class that doesn't implement anything. In the main method two objects of type Remote are created. The one with the reference variable of `screen1` is legal, but the one with the reference variable of `screen2` creates a compiler problem. Therefore, the following line of code executes without problems:

```
System.out.println(screen1.turnOn());
```

However, the following line creates a problem:

```
Remote screen2 = new Screen2();
```

The reason for this is since `screen2` does not implement the interface, it can't use `Remote` as a reference type. This can be corrected by making `Screen2` implement the `Remote` interface.

Extending interfaces

Interfaces typically contain abstract or unimplemented methods, but the reason why a developer may want to implement a method is to upgrade the interface. It's true that changing the code to the classes that implement an interface can be done without affecting anything, but the converse is not the same. Therefore, before Java 8 if a developer wanted to change the code to an interface then the classes that implement it will not reflect the changes and the code will break. This is not ideal if a software company upgrades the libraries that their clients rely on as if the clients utilize the new interface without rewriting their implementations then the code will break. One solution is to add `default` methods which guarantees binary compatibility with code written for older versions of the interfaces. In addition, `static` methods could also be implemented to be used as helper methods.

Default methods

To declare a default method in an interface use the following syntax:

```
default returnType methodName(parameter 1, parameter2,
...parameter n) {
 // body statements
}
```

An example of a default method in Java is written in the code snippet below:

```
default String test1() {
 return "";
}
```

A default method is not abstract; therefore you will have to specify a method body.

Extending interfaces that contain default methods

If a programmer extends an interface which contains default methods then they have three choices:

1) Ignore the default method which allows the extended class to inherit the default method.

2. Re-declare the default method which makes it `abstract`. An example of this is listed below:

```
interface InterfaceExample {

    default String test1() {

        return "";

    }


    static void test2() {

    }

}


public class TestOne implements InterfaceExample {

    public String test1() {

        return "";

    }

}
```

3) Override the default method by re-defining it. An example of this in Java is included below:

```
interface InterfaceExample {

    default String test1() {

        return "";
```

```
        }
    }
public class TestOne implements InterfaceExample {
    public String test1() {
        return "hello";
    }
}
```

Static methods in interfaces

As of Java 8, static methods can be implemented inside an interface. The syntax for doing so is listed below:

```
static returnType methodName(parameter1, parameter2, ...,
parameter n) {
  // body statements
}
```

An example of a bare bone static method in an interface is listed below:

```
static void test2() {
}
```

Static methods in interfaces are typically used as helper methods, or methods that return something that is used inside a more complex method. Remember, a static method is a method that's associated with the class it's defined in as opposed to any object. Therefore, this helps keep the helper methods in a library organized as the static methods inside an interface are specific to it as opposed to a separate class.

Interface example

Let's create an interface that allows us to compute the perimeter and area of a variety of shapes. The shapes that we want to do this for are Triangle, Square, and Parallelogram. The interface will be called Shapes, and contain two abstract methods which are perimeter()and area(). The classes that implement the interface will all define their own methods for perimeter and area since these shapes all have unique formulas. The sample interface is listed below:

Figure 5.10: Interface example. Shapes.java.

```java
public interface Shapes {

    double perimeter();

    double area();

}
```

As you can see in the above code snippet, the interface contains two methods which return a double.

The first class that implements it is `Triangle.java` which is displayed below:

Figure 5.11: A class that implements an interface.

```java
public class Triangle implements Shapes {

    private double a;

    private double b;

    private double c;

    double base;

    double height;

    public void setPerimeter(double a, double b,
    double c) {

        this.a = a;

        this.b = b;

        this.c = c;

    }

    public void setArea(double base, double height) {

        this.base = base;

        this.height = height;

    }

    public double perimeter() {

        double perimeter = a + b + c;

        return perimeter;
```

```
    }


    public double area() {

        double area = .5 * (base * height);

        return area;

    }

}
```

This class implements the perimeter and area methods that are specific to a triangle. All triangles have three sides, and the formula for computing the perimeter is to sum up all three sides. The formula for computing the area is ½ (base × height). Notice that `Triangle.java` contains fields and behaviors which are not included in `Shapes.java`. The reason for this is when a class implements an interface it essentially inherits that class's fields and behaviors. However, the subclass also has the option of including additional elements which are not found in the interface. The following class implements the `Shapes` interface for a `Parallelogram`. Note, the formula for calculating the perimeter for a Parallelogram is $P = 2(a + b)$, and the area is $A = bh$.

Figure 5.12: A class that implements an interface.

```
public class Parallelogram implements Shapes {

        private double a;

        private double b;

        private double base;

        private double height;


        public void setPerimeter(double a, double b) {

            this.a = a;

            this.b = b;

        }


        public double perimeter() {
```

```
        return 2 * (a + b);
    }


    public void setArea(double base, double height) {
        this.base = base;
        this.height = height;
    }


    public double area() {
        return base * height;
    }
}
```

Like `Triangle.java`, `Parallelogram.java` has its own version of `perimeter()` and `area()`. In addition, it also has fields and behaviors which are unique to its class. The following class implements `Shapes.java` for a Square class. The perimeter for a square is 4a, while the area is a2. The code is listed below:

Figure 5.13: A class that implements an interface. Square.java.

```
public class Square implements Shapes {
    private double a;
    public Square(double a) {
        this.a = a;
    }
    public double perimeter() {
        return 4 * a;
    }
    public double area() {
        return a * a;
    }
}
```

Below is the driver class which contains the main method and test the methods in the classes:

```java
public class ShapeShifter {

    public static void main(String[] args) {

        Triangle per = new Triangle();

        per.setPerimeter(10.0, 20., 30.0);

        System.out.println("The perimeter of triangle
        is " + per.perimeter());

        Triangle area = new Triangle();

        area.setArea(20, 50);

        System.out.println("The area of a traingle is
        " + area.area());

        Square sq = new Square(5);

        System.out.println("The perimeter of a square
        is " + sq.perimeter());

        sq.area();

        System.out.println("The area of a square is "
        + sq.area());

        Parallelogram par = new Parallelogram();

        par.setPerimeter(7.5, 8.1);

        System.out.println("The    perimeter    of    the
Parallelogram is " + par.perimeter());

        par.setArea(11.3, 9.9282);

        System.out.println("The area of the Parallel-
        ogram is " + par.area());

    }

}
```

The output is:

The perimeter of triangle is 60.0

The area of a triangle is 500.0

The perimeter of a square is 20.0

The area of a square is 25.0

The perimeter of the Parallelogram is 31.2

The area of the Parallelogram is 112.18866000000001

Abstract classes

According to dictionary.com, the word abstract means thought of apart from concrete realities, specific objects, or actual instances. If someone asks you to bring buy them something *tasty* from the grocery store, then something "tasty" is abstract because it's not clear. Something tasty could be pizza, sandwich, apple, or ice-cream? If someone said that they saw an *animal* in the zoo then that "animal" is abstract. Can it be giraffe, flamingo, or lion? Abstract ideas are concepts that must be visualized through concrete or real examples which are analogous to abstract classes in Java. An **abstract class** is a type of class that's declared with the `abstract` keyword, can't be instantiated, and can be extended.

The syntax for declaring an abstract class is listed below:

```
accessModifier abstract class ClassName {
 // statements
}
```

This syntax converted to actual Java code is listed below:

```
public abstract class Canine {
}
```

An `abstract` class must be `public` or package-private; it cannot be `private`. The purpose of an `abstract` class is to be extended by another class so if it was `private` this will prevent that from being possible. In addition, an `abstract` class cannot be `final`.

An `abstract` class may contain many of the behaviors and fields that are typical of a normal class such as: instance fields, static fields, methods, static methods, constructors, and abstract methods. A class just needs one `abstract` method in order for it to be considered abstract.

How are abstract classes different than regular classes?

One thing that sets `abstract` classes apart from regular classes is that it can never be instantiated. It serves as a general class for other classes, so it's typically extended by subclasses. You can declare `abstract` methods only in an `abstract` class. A normal class can't declare an `abstract` method without setting off a compile error.

In addition, you may be wondering why constructors are allowed for `abstract` classes if they can never be instantiated. Well, a reason for that is that the constructor is used to initialize fields. Remember, the constructor actually doesn't build the actually object, that's what the new keyword is for.

To make more sense of this here's some Java code:

Figure 5.14: abstract class demo.

```
public abstract class AbstractClass {

    private int a;

    private int b;


    public AbstractClass(int a, int b) {

        this.a = a;

        this.b = b;

    }


    public void addSum() {

        int sum = a + b;

        System.out.println(sum);

    }

}


public class AbstractTest extends AbstractClass {

    public AbstractTest() {
```

```
        super(5, 10);

}

public static void main(String[] args) {

        AbstractClass run = new AbstractClass();

        run.addSum();

}

}
```

The abstract class is named AbstractClass, and it contains two instance fields, a constructor which initializes the state of the object, and a method named addSum() that computes the sum of two numbers. The class that extends the abstract class is named AbstractTest, and it's a normal class that contains a constructor and a main method. Inside of the constructor is the super method which references the constructor of the super class. It passes the values of 5 and 10 into the AbstractClass constructor.

However, there's a problem. The code won't compile as a result of this snippet of code:

```
AbstractClass run = new AbstractClass();
```

Remember, you can't instantiate an abstract class so this will create a compile error. In order to fix this the following should be adjusted to state the following:

```
AbstractTest run = new AbstractTest();
```

In the above snippet, an object is crated of type AbstractTest which will make the compiler happy. When the method is invoked the following will be printed:

15

How are abstract classes different than interfaces?

If you're new to interfaces and abstract classes they may seem similar but with deeper research you'll discover that they have quite a few differences. Below are some observations about the differences between the two:

Only an interface can include default methods: While an abstract class can include instance and static methods, they're not allowed to contain default methods.

An interface can only have constants: Therefore, the default modifier for all variables in an interface is static final. This is not the case with abstract classes as they're more similar to concrete classes in this regard as they can include instance or static fields.

No modifiers in an interface: The methods and constants in an interface are assumed to be `abstract` and `static final` respectively so no modifiers are needed. An interface only allows the access modifiers of `public` or package-private on constants. Using `private` or `protected` will generate a compile error. This is not the case with an `abstract` class as not only do they allow instance variables and methods, but they allow them to have any modifiers. Therefore, the following snippets of code will compile inside an interface:

```
int a = 1;
```

```
public int b = 2;
```

However, the following snippets of code are all incorrect in an interface:

```
int a;
```

```
private int b = 2;
```

```
protected String b = "hey";
```

However, all the above snippets of code will compile without errors inside of an `abstract` class.

In addition, the following methods are legal inside an interface.

```
void getNumber();
```

```
public abstract void getName();
```

However, this is not the case with an `abstract` class. The method `getNumber()` is illegal in an abstract class because the modifiers of `public` and `abstract` are not assumed to be a part of the method declaration. A programmer must implicitly list the modifiers in order for it to be considered `abstract`. Otherwise, the compiler will be fetching for the body of `getNumber()` which it doesn't include. There are a couple of fixes to this problem. One, you could make the method `abstract` which is shown in the following snippet:

```
abstract void getNumber();
```

Or, you could provide a body for the method which is indicated below:

```
void getNumber() {

}
```

The `getName()` method is fine in the abstract class since it includes the keyword abstract in a method declaration which means that the method should be left unimplemented.

What interfaces do have in common with abstract classes is that you cannot create an instance of either one. The details of an interface are typically unimplemented, and the details of an abstract class are typically partially done. Therefore, these types of classes are typically used as a starting point and are extended and then modified by its subclasses.

When to use an abstract class over an interface?

Before trying to form a generic template on when to automatically use interfaces or abstract classes I would like to recommend to truly think about the features of both of them. An interface defines a contract between the classes that implements it. It states that any class that implements me must also extend my methods and share all my constants. However, an interface doesn't provide any specifications. Therefore, it's recommended to use interfaces when the functionality will be used across a wide spectrum of objects. Interfaces are great for providing common characteristics amongst unrelated classes. Even though an interface's methods are unimplemented they do enforce the parameters and return types, so if you want implemented methods to be forced into this then an interface is a good choice.

An abstract class on the other hand is kind of like a hybrid between an interface and a concrete or traditional class. It can contain abstract methods but it can also implement methods as well. Unlike interfaces which can be inherited from multiple classes an abstract class may only be inherited by a single class. Abstract classes are good choices if you want the classes to have shared functionality as its subclasses will contain its attributes and behaviors.

Abstract class example

If abstract classes are still well, abstract to you then maybe the following example will clarify things. I'm going to use canines as example since many people are familiar with them. Animals that are part of this family are domesticated dogs, coyotes, jackals, foxes, and wolves. I decided to use Canine as the super class for this example. Below is the abstract class for this example named Canine.java.

Figure 5.15: abstract class demo.

```
public abstract class Canine {
        static final int numOfLegs = 4;
```

```
public boolean haveCanineTeeth() { return true; }

abstract void getHabitat();

abstract void lifeSpan();

abstract boolean doBark();
}
```

This abstract class is not only the super class, but it serves as loose template for all of its subclasses. It contains one instance method called haveCanineTeeth() and three abstract methods named getHabitat(), lifeSpan(), and do-Bark(). The class also has one constant called numOfLegs which is set to 4. This makes sense in this context since all canines to my knowledge have four legs. Three additional classes are created that extends the super class called AfricanWild-Dog, Coyote, and Basenji and implements the methods in them in order to make the class specific as opposed to general.

The code for class AfricanWildDog is listed below:

Figure 5.16: abstract class demo.

```
public class AfricanWildDog extends Canine {

    public AfricanWildDog() {

        System.out.println("The \"AfricanWildDog\"
        class");

    }

    public void getHabitat() {

        System.out.println("Dense forest and open
        plains");

    }

    public boolean doBark() {

        return true;

    }

    public void lifeSpan() {

        System.out.println("10-15 years");

    }
```

}

The class has a constructor which prints the name of the class when called. It also implements the three abstract methods found in `Canine.java.` Failure to implement those abstract methods in the subclass would lead to a compile error.

The second subclass `Coyote` extends the `Canine` super class and is listed below:

Figure 5.17: abstract class demo.

```java
public class Coyote extends Canine {

    public Coyote() {

        System.out.println("The \"Coyote\" class");

    }


    public void getHabitat() {

        System.out.println("Desert, grasslands,
        foothills, to populated neighborhoods");

    }


    public boolean doBark() {

        return true;

    }


    public void lifeSpan() {

        System.out.println("10-14 years");

    }

}
```

Like the `AfricanWildDog` class it has a constructor that prints a statement when called, and overrides the abstract methods found in `Canine.java.` The next class is `Basenji,` and is listed below:

Figure 5.18: abstract class demo. Basenji.java.

```java
public class Basenji extends Canine {

    public Basenji() {

        System.out.println("The \"Basenji\" class");

    }

    public void getHabitat() {

        System.out.println("Natural habitat is
        forest regions of the Congo Basin");

    }

    public boolean doBark() {

        return false;

    }

    public void lifeSpan() {

        System.out.println("Median is 13.6 years");

    }

}
```

Like the previous two classes it provides a constructor and implements the three methods. It differs from the other two classes as the value returned in the method doBark() returns true as opposed to false. The reason for this is that the domesticated dog Basenji is not known for barking even though it does make vocalized sounds. CanineTest test the methods of each class.

```java
public class CanineTest {

    public static void main(String[] args) {

        Canine africanDog = new AfricanWildDog();

        africanDog.getHabitat();

        System.out.println(africanDog.doBark());

        africanDog.lifeSpan();

        System.out.println(africanDog.
        haveCanineTeeth());

        System.out.println("-----");
```

```
Canine coyote = new Coyote();
coyote.getHabitat();
System.out.println(coyote.doBark());
coyote.lifeSpan();
System.out.println("-----");
Canine basenji = new Basenji();
basenji.getHabitat();
System.out.println(basenji.doBark());
basenji.lifeSpan();
System.out.println(basenji.numOfLegs);
    }
}
```

The output is:

The "AfricanWildDog" class

Dense forest and open plains

true

10-15 years

true

The "Coyote" class

Desert, grasslands, foothills, to populated neighborhoods

true

10-14 years

The "Basenji" class

Natural habitat is forest regions of the Congo Basin

false

Median is 13.6 years

4

Nested classes

Java allows classes to be included inside other classes--this technique is called nested classes. An example of its syntax is listed below:

```
public class OuterName {

    // statements

    class NestedClass {

        // statements

    }

}
```

Before we dive into the technicalities of nested classes let's get a grasp of the terminology. There are two categories for nested classes which are static and non-static. Nested classes that are declared with the static modifier are called static nested classes while non-static nested classes are called inner classes.

Remember, they're both nested classes, but they're just two different types of flavors.

It's important to know that all nested classes are members of its enclosing class, or the class that it's located inside of. One main difference between static nested classes (ones declared with static modifier) and the non-static nested classes (inner classes) is that inner classes have access to all of the members of its enclosing (outside) classes even if they're declared `private`. An important distinguishing feature of nested classes vs. traditional classes is that nested classes can also be declared with the `private` or `protected` access modifiers. Remember, traditional classes can only be declared `public` or package-private, but this limitation is gone with an inner class. Therefore, the following syntax will compile without problems:

```
public class OuterClass {

    private int a;

    private double b;

    private float c;


    private class InnerClass {

        private int d;
```

```
        private double e;

        private String f;

    }

}
```

The benefits of nested classes

Nested classes are not there to make our code more confusing, they exist to do quite the opposite. Below are some reasons on when you may want to adapt nested classes in your programs:

Smart way to group classes: If a class is useful to another class, then it makes sense to embed that class into it.

Encapsulation: Imagine that you have two classes named X and Y. Class Y needs to access the fields of class X, but it can't because class X's fields are `private`. What's the workaround for this? One solution is to nest class Y inside of X because remember, a non-static nested class (inner class) can access the private members of its enclosing (outside) class. To further increase encapsulation class Y could also be hidden from the outside world as it can be declared `private`, `protected`, or package-private.

More maintainable code: If a program has many small classes, then spreading them out across separate java files could inflate the size of the codebase. An alternative solution is to analyze in which classes the smaller classes are associated with and see if they can be nested inside of the larger ones. This need to be done with caution as adding many nested classes into your code could make it more difficult for other programmers to grasp.

Static nested classes

A nested static class is associated with its outer class (the ones it's nested inside), kind of like the way that the variables and methods of a class are associated with the class it resides in. In addition, like static class methods, a static nested class can't refer directly to the instance variables or methods of its enclosing type. It can access them only through an object reference. It's important to state that static nested classes interact with instance members of outer classes the same way any top-level class would. It's correct to state that a static nested class is in essence a top-level class that has been nested within another top-level class.

Accessing members from static nested classes

To instantiate a static inner class use the following syntax:

```
OuterClass.InnerClass objectReference = new OuterClass.
InnerClass();
```

Here's a code snippet that shows a static inner class nested inside of an outer class, and instantiating an instance of the static inner class:

Figure 5.19: Outer class demo.

```
public class OuterClass {

    private int a;

    private double b;

    private float c;


    private static class StaticInnerClass {

        private static int d;

        private double e;

        private String f;

    }


    public static void main(String[] args) {

        OuterClass.StaticInnerClass test = new
        OuterClass.StaticInnerClass();

    }

}
```

Now that object is created, we can access the members of the inner class with the reference variable test.

```
test.d = 10;

System.out.println(test.d);

System.out.println(test.e);

test.f = "Static Inner Classes!";
```

```
System.out.println(test.f);
```

The following is printed:

10

0.0

Static Inner Classes!

Inner classes

Like instance variables and methods, an inner class is associated with an instance of a class. Therefore, an inner class may not include static members as that will generate compilation errors. An inner class has access to the outer class members because it exists within an instance of the outer class.

Accessing members from inner classes

To instantiate an inner class you must first instantiate the outer class, and then create an inner object within the outer object. The syntax for doing this is listed below:

```
OuterClass outerObject = new OuterClass();

OuterClass.InnerClass innerObject = outerObject.new

InnerClass();
```

Let's analyze some Java code to make more sense of this.

Figure 5.20: Outer class demo. Accessing members of an inner class.

```
public class OuterClass {

        private int a;

        private double b;

        private float c;


        private class InnerClass {

            private int getOuterInt() {

                return a;

            }
```

```
        private int d;

        private double e;

        private String f;

    }

    public static void main(String[] args) {

        OuterClass outer = new OuterClass();

        OuterClass.InnerClass inner = outer.new
        InnerClass();

        System.out.println(inner.d);

        System.out.println(inner.e);

        System.out.println(inner.f);

        System.out.println(inner.getOuterInt());

    }

}
```

The code contains two classes: one `public` outer class and one `private` inner class. The outer class contains three fields and the static method which execute print statements, and the inner class contains one `private` method and three fields. An instance of the outer class is created, and then its reference is used in the object creation of the inner class. Once the inner class is created it can access the members of its class with its reference variable which is inner. Remember, an inner class can reference the members of an outer class but it can't do so through its own reference variable. For example the following snippet of code will generate an error as it's not a property of the inner object:

```
System.out.println(inner.a);
```

However, you can create an accessor method in the inner class to return the fields that you want to access from the outer class. This is why the access method was added, and therefore is printed successfully.

There are two types of inner classes which are local classes and anonymous classes.

Local classes

Java allows classes to be included within methods and these types of classes are known as Local Classes. Just like how local variables are limited to the block in which they're written the same concept applies to local classes. However, a main distinction between local classes and variables is that local classes may also access members outside of it.

Below is a demo class for testing some of the features of a local class:

Figure 5.21: Local class demo.

```java
public class LocalClassDemo {
    // outer class instance fields
    private int a = 5;
    private int b = 10;
    private double c = 12.356;

    public void doCalculations(int a, int b) {
        // inner local class
        class Compute {
            int d;
            void getInt() {
                System.out.println(a + b);
            }
        }
        // instance of inner local class
        Compute compute = new Compute();
        compute.getInt();
    }

    public static void main(String[] args) {
        // instance of outer class
        LocalClassDemo demo = new LocalClassDemo();
        System.out.println(demo.a);
```

```
System.out.println(demo.b);

System.out.println(demo.c);

demo.doCalculations(1, 1);

    }

}
```

The outer class is called `LocalClassDemo`. It has three instance fields and a method called `doCalculations()` which accepts two parameters of type `int`. Inside the method is a local class called `Compute()`. That call contains a method which sums the values of the parameters of the `doCalculations()` method. Inside the `doCalculations()` method is an instance of the inner class which invokes the method. However, the method won't be run until the `doCalculations()` method is invoked. This happens in the last line of the main method.

The following is printed when the main method is invoked:

5

10

12.356

2

Anonymous classes

An anonymous class is an inner class that doesn't have a name, hence it being called anonymous. They're in essence an expression included within larger expressions like a method invocations. The syntax for creating anonymous classes in Java is a little unconventional so let's get acquainted with it before fiddling with code.

The syntax for creating anonymous classes

The components for anonymous classes typically consist of the following elements:

- The new operator.

- The name of the class to extend the super class or implement the interface.

- Parenthesis which contains the arguments in the constructor. When an interface is implemented empty parenthesis are used.

- A body which is similar to a class declaration. Remember, body statements are included between curly braces {}. Method declarations are allowed but statements are not.

The important thing to remember about the syntax of anonymous classes is that it's a small expression included within a statement.

For example, the syntax for creating an anonymous class is listed below:

```
ClassName referenceVariable = new ClassName() {

  // statements

};
```

Note, up until this point you're probably not accustomed to seeing semi colons dangling outside of curly braces. In this context it's needed as excluding it will provide a compile error that states the following:

```
error: ';' expected
```

In the above example, analyze the statement in which the object is created. After looking carefully you'll notice that it's not terminated by a semicolon. Instead, it includes curly braces which are where the statements of the inner class go between. The semi colon is needed in order to terminate the statement in which the expression for the anonymous class was added. An example of this translated into Java code is listed below:

Figure 5.22: Anonymous class demo.

```
public class Candy {

    public double getCost() {

        return 0.0;

    }

    Candy candyBar = new Candy() {

        public double getCost() {

            return 2.50;

        }

    };

}
```

When to use anonymous classes

At first glance, anonymous classes may seem like a pointless feature in Java but they do have their uses. Use anonymous classes to:

- Make your code more concise.

- To declare and instantiate a class simultaneously.

- If you need to use a local class just once.

Class diagrams

Most production software contains large codebases and thousands of lines of code spread out over many files. It's difficult for a new developer to join a software team and quickly make sense of it as there are simply too many pieces to the puzzle. If a new developer dives headfirst into the codebase then there's a possibility that they may become overwhelmed. There have been research studies conducted as far back as the 70s that assert that pictorial illustrations help improve students' learning from text (Russell N. Carney, Joel R Levin). In addition, this theory was validated as research conducted in the 90s has confirmed these findings. The concept of learning through images has been adapted to help diagram software, and is known as the Unified Modeling Language or UML for short. UML is a general purpose method for visualizing the design of a system. It was standardized by the Object Management Group (OMG) in 1997 and was made an ISO standard back in 2005.

This basic tutorial will equip you with the syntax of the modeling language by providing simple snippets of code accompanied by an associated diagram. Learning how to construct diagrams could be helpful for a software team, but remember that UML is simply a tool used for communication. Like all tools it's more useful when used situational, as doing so otherwise may lead to undesirable results. UML is a very large modeling language and there are literally books written about it. Therefore, I'm going to focus on a portion of it which is commonly used in object oriented design and analysis which are class diagrams.

Class diagram through example

Let's imagine that you've been hired by a large manufacturing company called *Macro Microwaves LLC,* and the first day on the job they want you to build a Java program that programmatically models the behavior of one of their microwaves. They plan to analyze your software to research ways that they can improve their product as their last quarter earnings were less than stellar. They request for your program to be object oriented and that you provide a complimentary class diagram when you demo or present your code. They also request for you to have this done by the end of the working day. They provide you some general requirements of the microwave in the form of use cases. A **use case** is a technique used in software engineering to list the actions or steps required to achieve a goal. There are no standard for defining use cases as many companies use varying formats. Below is a simplified version of a use case.

Use case number: 1
Use case name: heat
Description: Can defrost or reheat food depending on in which option the consumer chooses.

Need to be able to defrost from 1-4 lbs of food, and need to reheat pasta, meat, and vegetables.

Use case number: 2
Use case name: cancel
Description: Cancels the cook time inside a microwave. Sets time equal to zero.

Use case number: 3
Use case name: viewCookTime
Description: Displays the current cook time in the microwave

Use case number: 4
Use case name: turnTable
Description: Displays "on" if the on button is pushed and "off" if the off button is pushed.

Use case number: 5
Use case name: surfaceLight
Description: Turns surface light on if the "on" button is pushed and off if the "off" button is pushed.

Use case number: 6
Use case name: microwavePopcorn
Description: Convenience cooking feature that microwaves popcorn when the microwave popcorn is pushed by consumer.

Use case number: 7
Use case name: microwavePotato
Description: Convenience cooking feature that microwaves a potato when the microwave potato button is pushed by consumer.

Use case number: 8
Use case name: addTime

Description: An express cooking feature that allows the consumer to add 30 seconds or one through six minutes of extra time to the cook time.

Let's convert each use case into java code step-by-step. We'll also introduce the class diagrams along the way.

The first class I'm going to create is an interface called `Microwave.java.` The reason why this is done is because in use case number 1, there's a heat feature that can defrost or reheat food in the microwave. Therefore, there's a need for two different implementations for this function which is an appropriate time to use an interface. The code snippet for it is included below:

```
public interface Microwave {

        void heat(int heat);

}
```

The syntax for this code translated into a UML class diagram is listed below:

Figure 5.23: Interface example in a class diagram.

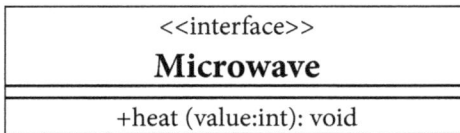

<<interface>>   **Microwave**
+heat (value:int): void

As you can see classes are represented in UML as rectangles that contain three rows. The first row is where the name of the class goes, the second row is for the attributes, and the third row is for operations. In order to label a class as an interface include the text <<interface>> above the class name. The typical convention for labeling a method in a UML diagram is as follows:

```
accessModifier methodName(arg list) : return type
```

In this example it translates to: `+heat(value:int):void`

Use (+) for `public` members, minus (-) for `private` members, hash (#) for `protected` members, and tilde (~) for package-private ones.

The next class I'm going to create is the Options one. This class will be declared `abstract` as I want the ability to add abstract methods to it in the future. In addition, it will also contain methods that will be shared with the classes that inherit it. Therefore, this class implements use cases 2-5. The code for the class is listed below:

Figure 5.24: The main abstract class.

```
public abstract class Options {
```

```java
protected double cookTime;


public void cancel() {
    this.cookTime = 0;
}


public void viewCookTime() {
    System.out.println(cookTime);
}


protected String turnTable(int button) {
    String state = "";
    if (button != 0 || button != 1)
        state = "enter valid input";
    if (button == 0) {
        state = "off";
    } else if (button == 1) {
        state = "on";
    }
    return state;
}


protected String surfaceLight(String button) {
    String state = "";
    if (button == "on") {
        state = "on";
    } else if (button == "off") {
```

```
        state = "off";

    }

    return state;

}

}
```

The code translated into a class diagram below.

Figure 5.25: Class diagram for Options.java.

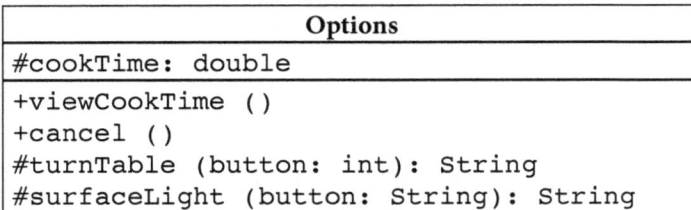

Options
#cookTime: double
+viewCookTime ()   +cancel ()   #turnTable (button: int): String   #surfaceLight (button: String): String

To indicate that a class is abstract in UML you *italicize* the name of the class.

The next class will model the convenience cooking features of the microwave. It translates use cases 6 and 7 into Java as it codes the microwavePopcorn() and microwavePotato() methods. In addition, since it implements the interface it creates its own version of the heat() method which is use case 1. In this version it heats food based on the servings in pounds. It also extends the Options class so it can use its methods if needed.

Figure 5.26: ConvenienceCooking.java.

```
public class ConvenienceCooking extends Options imple-
ments Microwave {

    @Override

    public void heat(int servingInPounds) {

        switch (servingInPounds) {

        case 1:

            cookTime += 8;

            System.out.println("Defrosting 1 lb of
            food");

            break;
```

```
        case 2:
                cookTime += 16;
                System.out.println("Defrosting 2 lbs of
                food");
                break;
        case 3:
                cookTime += 24;
                System.out.println("Defrosting 3 lbs of
                food");
                break;
        case 4:
                cookTime += 32;
                System.out.println("Defrosting 4 lbs of
                food");
                break;
        default:
                System.out.println("Enter number of
                servings in pounds: Options are 1-4");
        }
    }
    protected double microwavePopcorn() {
        cookTime += 3.30;
        return 3.30;
    }
    protected double microwavePotato() {
        cookTime += 7.00;
        return 7.00;
    }
}
```

Note, in order to implement the interface and extend a class, the **extends** keyword must come before the **implements** one. Doing this in reverse would generate a compile error. For example, the following code would not work.

```
public class ConvenienceCooking implements Microwave
extends Options.
```

The above code translated into a class diagram is indicated below:

Figure 5.27: ConvenienceCooking.java class diagram.

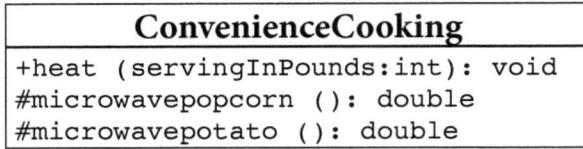

ConvenienceCooking
+heat (servingInPounds:int): void #microwavepopcorn (): double #microwavepotato (): double

However, this class has relationships with two other classes as it implements the interface and extends the abstract class.

This symbol indicates that a class implements another one.

This symbol indicates inheritance.

Here's how the updated class diagram looks:

Figure 5.28: Class diagram. Interface, inheritance, and implementation.

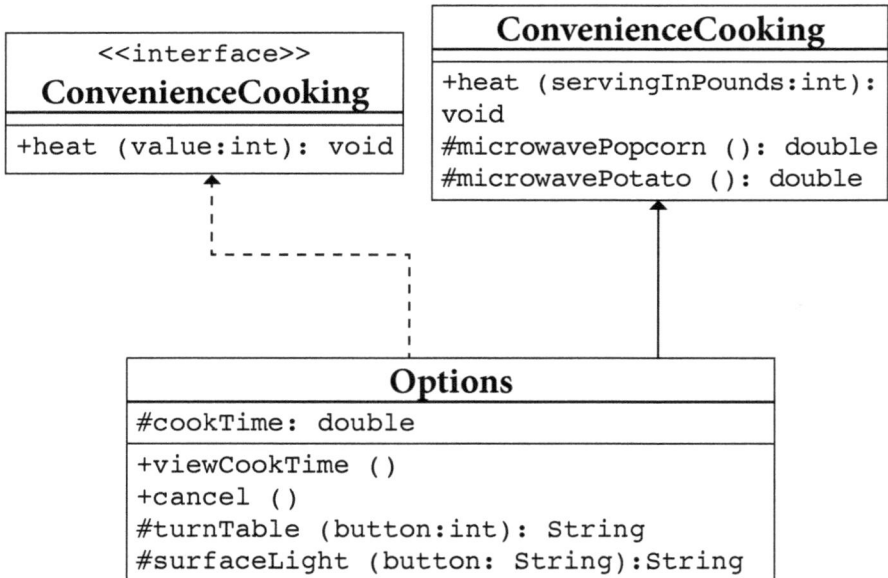

<<interface>> ConvenienceCooking
+heat (value:int): void

ConvenienceCooking
+heat (servingInPounds:int): void #microwavePopcorn (): double #microwavePotato (): double

Options
#cookTime: double
+viewCookTime () +cancel () #turnTable (button:int): String #surfaceLight (button: String):String

The next class will code the express cooking features which we'll call `ExpressCook`.

java. It codes use case 8 which allows the consumer to add more time to the current cook time, and it also implements its own version of the heat() method which is in use case 1. The difference between the heat method in ExpressCook compared to the one in ConvenienceCooking, is that the one in ExpressCook allows the consumer to reheat their food while the one in ConvenienceCooking allows the consumer to defrost their food by entering the serving size in pounds.

This class coded in Java is indicated below:

Figure 5.29: ExpressCook.java.

```
public class ExpressCook extends Options implements
Microwave {

    @Override
    public void heat(int reheat) {
        switch (reheat) {
        case 1:
            cookTime += 1;
            System.out.println("reheating 1 serving
            of pasta");
            break;
        case 2:
            cookTime += 8;
            System.out.println("reheating 1 serving
            of meat");
            break;
        case 3:
            cookTime += 3;
            System.out.println("reheating 1 serving
            of veggies");
            break;
        default:
            System.out.println("Enter type of food
            one serving:\n" + "1: pasta 2: meat 3:
            veggies");
```

```
        }
}
public void addTime(int time) {
        double add = 0.0;
        switch (time) {
        case 1:
                cookTime += 1;
                break;
        case 2:
                cookTime += 2;
                break;
        case 3:
                cookTime += 3;
                break;
        case 4:
                cookTime += 4;
                break;
        case 5:
                cookTime += 5;
                break;
        case 6:
                cookTime += 6;
                break;
        case 30:
                cookTime = (double) (time += add) / 100;
                // converts int to double
                break;
        default:
```

```
System.out.println("Enter cook time of
30 seconds, or 1-6 minutes");
    }
  }
}
```

The class translated into UML is indicated in the image below:

Figure 5.30: ExpressCook.java class diagram.

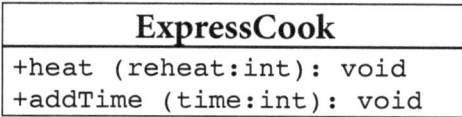

ExpressCook
+heat (reheat:int): void
+addTime (time:int): void

Since the class implements the interface and extends Options.java, these re-lationships should be reflected in the class diagram as well. The completed class diagram for this group of classes is listed below:

Figure 5.31: Completed class diagrams.

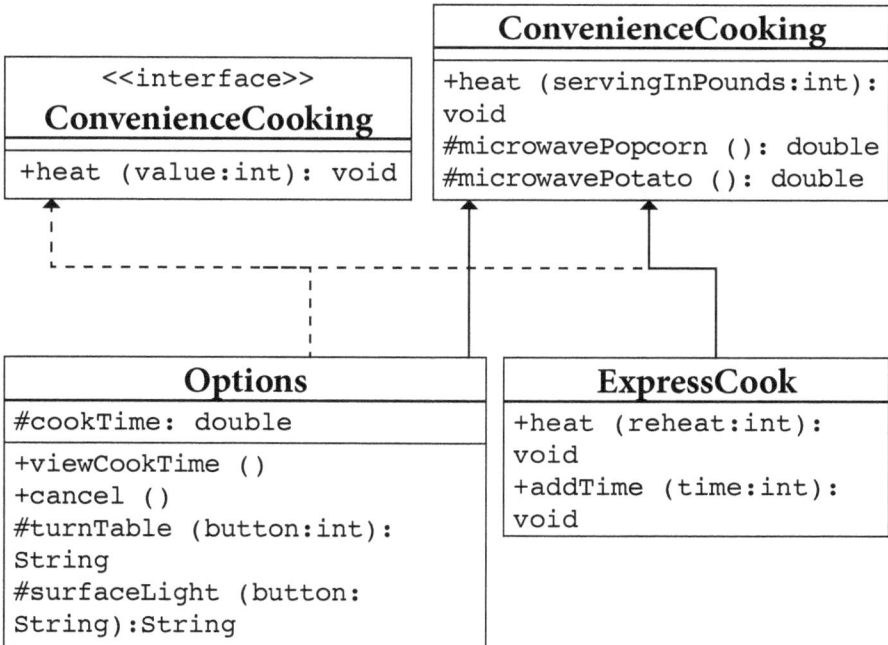

We'll need to create a class to test the functionality of the classes. The class we'll create is called MicrowaveTest.java and is indicated in the code below:

```java
public class MicrowaveTest {

    public static void main(String[] args) {

        ConvenienceCooking food = new
        ConvenienceCooking();

        // prints 0

        food.viewCookTime();

        System.out.println(food.turnTable(1));

        // prints on

        System.out.println(food.surfaceLight("on"));

        // prints on

        food.heat(3);

        food.microwavePopcorn();

        food.microwavePotato();

        // displays total cook time

        food.viewCookTime();

        // sets cook time equal to 0

        food.cancel();

        // displays total cook time

        food.viewCookTime();

        System.out.println("-------");

        ExpressCook express = new ExpressCook();

        express.addTime(30);

        express.viewCookTime();

        express.heat(1);

        express.heat(2);

        express.heat(3);

        // prints an error message
```

```
        express.heat(4);

        // displays total cook time

        express.viewCookTime();

    }

}
```

Here's the output form when the class is run:

0.0

on

on

Defrosting 3 lbs of food

34.3

0.0

0.3

reheating 1 serving of pasta

reheating 1 serving of meat

reheating 1 serving of veggies

Enter type of food one serving:

1: pasta 2: meat 3: veggies

12.3

Chapter 5 Re-factored

In this chapter you learned about the advanced topics based around object orientated programming such as inheritance and polymorphism. You also learned about a variety of different classes available in Java such as interfaces, abstract, inner, nested, local, and anonymous. You also learned about the unified modeling language (UML) and how to convert your Java code into class diagrams. A lot of topics were thrown at you in this chapter so if it all doesn't stick with you don't stress out. Try re-reading the chapter and working through the code to strengthen your comprehension. Also, I would highly recommend modeling real world objects that you're interested in into Java using oop techniques. Are you fascinated by airplanes, supercars, hover boards, drones, rocket ships, or smart watches? Try modeling basic features of these objects into Java code. You'll stay engaged in the process since you're working with objects that you're interested in, and you'll also deepen your oop knowledge.

Chapter 5 Resources

Dia Diagam Editor: http://dia-installer.de

Pictorial Illustrations Still Improve Students' Learning from Text: http://link.springer.com/article/10.1023/A:1013176309260

Scrum and agile project management book: (Scrum Magic) https://www.amazon.com/Scrum-Magic-Ultimate-Training-Framework/dp/0997326212

Chapter 5 Exercises

1)   T or F: The process in which a class acquires the properties of another class is known as extension.

2)   T or F: The class that inherits the properties of another class is called the super class.

3)   T or F: Abstraction and encapsulation are synonymous.

4)   T or F: Encapsulation can be defined as revealing only the necessary details to the user.

5)   T or F: Abstraction can be defined as hiding properties and methods.

6)   T or F: The super keyword allows you to call a constructor in the super class.

7)   T or F: The this keyword allows you to call a constructor in a child class.

8)   T or F: Interfaces allow abstraction.

9)   T or F: Including at least one abstract method in a class automatically makes it abstract.

10)   T or F: When a class implements an interface it inherits that class's attributes and methods.

11)   T or F: Methods in an interface can never be implemented.

12) T or F: Classes can't be nested inside each other.

13) T or F: Classes can't be private.

14) T or F: A class can extend at most one class.

15) T or F: A class can implement multiple classes.

Chapter 5 Exercise Answers

1) False. It's known as inheritance.

2) False. It's typically called the subclass, but it's also referred to as the child class.

3) False. They're related but different.

4) False. This is the definition of abstraction.

5) False. This is the definition of encapsulation.

6) True.

7) False. It allows you to call a different constructor in the same class

8) True. It hides the implementation details.

9) True.

10) True. A class can also implement multiple interfaces.

11) False. As of Java 8 default methods can be added to interfaces.

12) False. They can and they're known as nested classes.

13) False. They can if they're nested inside another class.

14) True. Trying to extend more than one class will lead to a compile error.

15) True.

Chapter 6: Strings

Strings are an important concept in programming languages as there needs to be a way to manipulate text in programs. In the previous chapters we were already introduced to Strings, some of its features, and even some of the methods for manipulating text such as `System.out.println()`. However, our knowledge about Strings up until this point has been superficial as we only had a narrow understanding about this feature in Java. Since we now understand some important concepts that are related to Strings such as objects, we'll now dig deeper to increase our sphere of knowledge about this concept. We're going to learn about the different ways to create Strings, how to manipulate them, and then take a tour of the String class available to us from the Java API.

How to declare Strings

A String can be defined as a sequence of characters enclosed within double quotation marks (""). Strings are related to but not equal to chars which are enclosed within single quotation marks ("). Up until this point we have been declaring Strings using the following notation:

```
String name = "Doug";
```

However, there's an alternative way to create a String in Java as indicated in the following code snippet:

```
String name = new String("Doug");
```

The next question is what are the differences between the different ways to declare Strings in Java? The differences are subtle and it's better explained by analyzing snippets of code.

Look at the following:

```
String name1 = "Doug";

String name2 = "Doug";

boolean test = name1 == name2;

System.out.println(test);
```

The output for this snippet of code is true. What happens is two String variables are created which points to the String literal Doug.

Now, we're going to make one minor tweak to the existing code. Instead of creating a String literal we're going to use the new operator with a constructor to create a String object. The updated code is listed below:

```
String name1 = new String("Doug");

String name2 = new String("Doug");

boolean test = name1 == name2;

System.out.println(test);
```

The output for this snippet is false. The next question is but how? What happens in the latter example is that the == operator compares the two object references which are not the same. Since two different objects are created, they have two different locations in memory. Comparing references is not the same as comparing the value, which is why the second example prints false.

Let's analyze the following code snippet:

```
String name1 = "Doug";

String name2 = "Doug";
```

If there are 100 "Doug" String literals in a program then there will only be one copy of it in memory. Each variable will reference it through a process called String interning. This process is similar to caching as when the String literal is created it's held a prisoner in Java memory. Therefore, there will never be two copies of the same String literal in memory, as each of them must be unique. Before JDK 7 String literals were sent to a special area reserved inside the heap known as Permanent Generation, but as of Java 8 the Permanent Generation area has been removed and all String literals are stored on the heap. When a String literal is created, the intern() method is invoked. Therefore, if we call the intern() method on a String object we can internalize it which makes it a String literal as indicated in the code snippet below:

```
test = name1.intern() == name2.intern();
```

The result of this when printed is `true`.

Strings are considered immutable in Java as once an object is created it cannot under normal circumstances be modified.

How to compare Strings

In the String class in the Java api there's a method called equals()which allows you to compare one object to another. Let's update the code in the previous example to state the following:

```
String name1 = new String("Doug");

String name2 = new String("Doug");

System.out.println(name1.equals(name2));
```

The output in this example is: `true`

What makes the `equals()` method different from (==) is that the latter analyzes the reference to the object while the `equals()` method analyzes the actual value which is what you want. In addition, the `equals()` method can also be used on String literals, so the following code snippet is legal:

```
boolean test = "Hello".equals("Hello");

System.out.println(test);
```

The output of this is `true`.

Concatenation

Concatenation is a fancy word that means the joining of Strings. When the plus operator (+) is used in the context of Strings it means to concatenate instead of arithmetic. For example, the following code snippet shows the concatenation of Strings:

```
System.out.print("I'm on a seafood diet." + "I see food
" + "and I eat it.");
```

The output is: `I'm on a seafood diet. I see food and I eat it.`

The String Class in the Java API also provides the `concat()` method which duplicates this functionality.

The method is used in the following code snippet:

```
System.out.println("With great power comes
".concat("great electricity bill"));
```

The output is: With great power comes great electricity bill

Even though this feature is available in the API, the + operator is more commonly used.

Multiple line spans

Java prohibits the use of a single String that spans multiple lines. Therefore, the following code snippet is not permitted:

```
System.out.println("Lorem     ipsum     dolor     sit     amet,
consectetuer adipiscing elit. Aenean commodo ligula eget
dolor. Aenean massa. Cum sociis natoque penatibus et
magnis dis parturient montes, nascetur ridiculus mus.");
```

To correct this break the text into multiple Strings. For example, the following code snippet will compile without errors.

```
System.out.println("Lorem     ipsum     dolor     sit     amet,
consectetuer adipiscing elit." + "Aenean commodo ligula
eget dolor. Aenean massa. Cum sociis natoque penatibus
et magnis" + "dis parturient montes, nascetur ridiculus
mus.");
```

Printing mixed types

Java allows programmers to print text consisting of varying types. An example that prints an int, String, char, boolean, and double is listed below:

```
System.out.println(1 + " is an integer." + " Hi " + "is a
String. " + 'A' + " is a char. " + true + " is a boolean.
" + 1.11 + " is a double.");
```

The output for this is: 1 is an integer. Hi is a String. A is a char. true is a boolean. 1.11 is a double.

However, the PrintStream class in the Java api provides two methods for formatting the text of strings which are: printf() and printformat(). Let's look at the method summary for each which is taken from the Java api:

```
PrintStream printf(String format, Object... args)
```

For example, the following code prints the statement 1 is an integer:

```
System.out.println(1 + " is an integer");
```

However, the `printf` method can also be used as well and the code snippet for printing the equivalent would be as follows:

```
System.out.printf("%d is an integer", 1);
```

In the above code snippet %d is known as a format specifier and when it's included in the String it tells the compiler to look for a decimal integer. Below is a table for format specifiers that's allowed in the `printf()` method.

Figure 6.0: Table of format specifiers.

%d	Displays integers
%f	Displays floating points
%e or %E	Displays floating points in exponential notation
%c or %C	Displays characters
%s or %S	Displays Strings
%b or %B	Displays booleans
%%	Displays a % sign

Here's the previous example formatted with the `printf()` method:

```
System.out.printf("%d" + " is an integer. " + "%s" + " is a
String. " + "%c" + " is a char. " + "%b" + " is a boolean. "
+ "%f" + " is a double.", 1,"hi",'A',true,1.11);
```

When the format() method is used the output is the same. For example, this produces the same output as the above snippet:

```
System.out.format("%d" + " is an integer. " + "%s" + " is
a String. " + "%c" + " is a char. " + "%b" + " is a boolean.
" + "%f" + " is a double.", 1,"hi",'A',true,1.11);
```

In addition, the String class has its own version of the `format()` method. Its method details is as follows: `public static String format(String format, Object... args)`

An example of it being used is:

```
System.out.println(String.format("%d %d %f", 1,2,3.0));
```

Escape characters

Java provides a myriad of escape characters which provides more ways for developers to format text. The following table lists the escape codes with an associated short description.

Figure 6.1: Table of escape characters.

Escape Sequence	Description
\t	Inserts a tab at this point
\b	Inserts a backspace at this point
\n	Inserts a newline at this point
\r	Inserts a carriage return at this point
\f	Inserts a form feed at this point
\'	Inserts a single quote at this point
\"	Inserts a double quote at this point
\\	Inserts a backslash at this point

The following code snippet shows the tab escape being implemented in order to create tabulated data.

```
String column = "";

column += "Month\t" + "Day\t" + "Year\t\n";

column += "-----\t" + "---\t" + "----\n";

column += "Feb\t" + "1st\t" + "2050\t";

System.out.println(column);
```

The output is:

```
Month     Day        Year

-----     ---        ----

Feb       1st        2050
```

The following code snippet shows the newline escape being implemented:

```
String line1 = "first\n";

String line2 = "second";

System.out.print(line1 + line2);
```

The output is:

first

second

The following code snippet shows the double quotation escape being applied:

```
String title = "\"Of Mice and Men\"";

System.out.println(title);
```

The output is: "Of Mice and Men"

Analyzing the String class in java

The String class in Java 8 has 15 constructors and 67 methods. We're going to analyze some of the methods in order to gain a better understanding of what's available to us developers.

Char charAt(int index)

This method returns a char at the specified index. You must enter an integer as a parameter. Below is an example code snippet that shows how the method works:

```
String phase = "at night i can't sleep in the morning I cannot wake up";

char result = phase.charAt(4);

System.out.println(result);
```

The output is i.

public int compareTo(String anotherString)

This method requires a String parameter and returns an int. It compares two Strings lexicographically and returns a negative number of this String object lexicographically precedes the argument String. The result is positive if the String object lexicographically follows the argument String. It returns a 0 if the two Strings are equal. The following code snippet shows the compareTo() method in action:

```
String s1 = "hi";

String s2 = "hi";
```

```
int result = s1.compareTo(s2);

System.out.println(result);
```

The result printed is 0.

public boolean startsWith(String prefix, int toffset)

This method compares two Strings and checks to see if the substring appears in the String at the specified index. If it does then the method returns true, if not then the method returns false.

Here's the method being used in action:

```
String planet = "Mars";

boolean test = planet.startsWith("Ma",0);

System.out.println(test);
```

The following prints true.

boolean endsWith(String suffix)

This method tests to see if a String ends with a certain index. The method is used in the following code snippet:

```
boolean test = "Guitar".endsWith("r");

System.out.println(test);
```

The result printed is true.

int hashCode()

This method returns the hash code for a String. Every object has a `hashCode()` method, and most classes includes in the Collection API should implement their own `hashcode()` method. The method in action is indicated in the snippet below:

```
System.out.println("Hello".hashCode());
```

The output is: 69609650

indexOf()

The Java api provides four overrides for the indexOf()method. These methods are useful if you want to search a String for a certain characters. In the following example we'll impellent this version of the method:

public int indexOf(int ch)

```
int result = "Brouhaha".indexOf('a');

System.out.println(result);
```

The output is: 5

The parameter of the method is int ch which is short for char. Remember, a char in Java is an integral type so passing it into the parameter is legal.

boolean isEmpty()

This boolean analyzes the length of a String and returns true if the length is 0, and 1 if its false. Below is the method in action.

```
boolean result = "Collywobbles".isEmpty();

System.out.println(result);
```

The result that's printed is: 0

valueOf()

This method accepts in any object and returns the String representation of it. Since its a static method it has to be invoked in the format of: String.valueof()

An example of the method being implemented is listed below:

```
String s = String.valueOf(123);

System.out.println(s);
```

The output is 123.

To confirm that the output is indeed a String lets run a little test. We can add a number to the String and the output should also be a String. Let's assume that this statement is added underneath the previous print statement.

```
System.out.println(s + 2);
```

The output is: 1232

Therefore, the conversion from an int to String is verified.

length()

This method returns the length of a String as an int.

```
int length = "donnybrook".length();

System.out.println(length);
```

The output is: 10

Note, empty spaces also count as characters which is null. For example, the previous code has been updated in the following snippet:

```
int length = "donnybrook".length();

System.out.println(length);
```

The output in this case is now 11.

replace(char oldChar, char newChar)

This method replaces all occurrences of the char in the String with occurrences of the new char. An example of the code being implemented is listed below:

```
String update = "flibbertigibbet".replace("f", "");

System.out.println(update);
```

The output is: libbertigibbet

String [] split(String regex)

This method splits the String around the match given by the regular expression. It accepts a String and returns an array of Strings. The following code snippet shows this method in action:

```
String[] update = "fuddy-duddy".split("-");

for (int i = 0; i < update.length; i++) {

  System.out.print(update[i]);

}
```

The output is: fuddyduddy

String substring(int beginIndex)

This method returns a substring of this String beginning at the specified index. An example of this method being used is listed below:

```
String sub = "Gazump".substring(2);

System.out.println(sub);
```

The output is: zump

String toLowercase()

This method converts the String into all lowercase. If you pass in a String with all lowercase then the output would be identical. The following code snippet shows this method in action:

```
String caps = "HOOSEGOW".toLowerCase();

System.out.println(caps);
```

The output is: hoosegow

String toUpperCase()

This method returns a String converted into all uppercase. An example of the method implemented is listed below:

```
String upper = "kerfuffle".toUpperCase();

System.out.println(upper);

Th e output is: KERFUFFLE
```

trim()

This method returns a String whose value remains the same with the exception of leading or trailing whitespace removed. The code snippet below shows the method in action:

```
System.out.println(" Hi there   ".trim());
```

The output is:

Hi there

Without the trim() method the text would be distorted.

Chapter 6 Re-factored

This chapter provided a quick overview about Strings in Java. Strings are actually an object, and can be created by using a String literal or the new operator. Strings are immutable, and once you create them that literal will remain in the heap. The String class provides a *buffet* of methods that developers can utilize in their programs in order to speed up the development process. Memorizing all of the methods would be difficult and counterproductive. Instead, try and memorize the methods that you find yourself using often. If you don't have much experience with programming then study Java programs that deal with Strings and keep note of which methods from the String Class that's used often. Some popular methods are `length()`, `trim()`, `toUpperCase()`,`toLowerCase()`,`startWith()`,`endsWith()`, and `replace()`.

Chapter 6 Resources

String Class: https://docs.oracle.com/javase/8/docs/api/java/lang/String.html

Chapter 6 Exercises

1. T or F: A String is considered immutable in Java.

2. T or F: The value that's printed in the following snippet is null.

    ```
    String test = "";

    System.out.println(test);
    ```

3. T or F: A String is a primitive type like an `int` or `double`.

4. T or F: The String class is not final in Java

5. T or F: The String class does not extend the Object class in Java.

6. T or F: A String is considered a type of Object in Java.

7. T or F: The following code snippet compiles without errors in Java.

    ```
    Object y = new String("y");
    ```

8. T or F: The following code snippet is valid:

    ```
    Object x = "name";
    ```

```
System.out.println(x);
```

9. 9. What does the following code print?

```
String s = "Hello";

boolean truth = s instanceof Object;

System.out.println(truth);
```

10. What does the following code print?

```
String test1 = new String("Hey");

String test2 = "Hey";

boolean truth = test1.equals(test2);

System.out.println(truth);
```

11. Answer the questions regarding the following snippet of code:

```
String original = "Skedaddle";

String change = "Skullduggery";

original = change;

System.out.println(original);
```

   a) Are Strings mutuable in Java?

   b) What's printed?

   c) How many String objects were created in this code?

Chapter 6 Answers

1) True. Once it's created it cannot be changed. However, multiple references to the String literal can be made.

2) False. An empty space is printed.

3) False. A String is a reference type.

4) False. It's declared final in the Java api.

5) False. All classes in Java extend the Object class whether implicitly or explicitly.

6)   True. Strings are objects and are considered reference types as opposed to primitive types.

7)   True. Since Strings are a type of Object the following code snippet is valid.

8)   True. The result it prints is name.

9)   True. Since String is an instance of Object the boolean returns true.

10)   True. The equals() method compares the value as opposed to the references.

11)

    a)   No.

    b)   Skullduggery

    c)   Two. Each String creates their own object. When the third statement is executed the first variable is referencing the second one.

Chapter 7 Arrays

Ever ate a box of Valentines chocolates? If so, then you're in luck as it will help illustrate the concepts of arrays. Arrays are a special kind of object in Java that can hold primitive or reference types. An array may store varying amounts of the same data type at certain locations. Kind of like how in certain spots in the box of chocolates you may have varying quantities or sizes of chocolates. In addition, the box of chocolates will typically list the count or the number of chocolates inside of it. This is analogous to the concept of arrays as they have a `length` property which reveals the total number of elements in it. In this chapter we'll explore the features of arrays so that we can start incorporating them into our programs.

The law of arrays

There are two ways that you can create arrays in Java. You can create an array literal or you can use the new operator to create an array object. Below is the syntax that you would use to create an array literal:

```
type[] arrayName = {value1,value2,vaue3,…valuen};
```

An example of this translated to Java is listed below:

Figure 7.1: Array creation example.

```
int[] evenNumbers = {2,4,6,8,10};
```

What this does is create an array of integers. An array can be either a primitive or a reference type. If the array is a primitive than the maximum number it can hold is equal to the maximum value of its type. For example, the above code snippet is an array of ints, therefore the maximum number that it can hold is $2^{32} - 1$, or 2147483647.

An array could also be constructed using the new operator. The syntax that you would use to do this is listed below:

```
type[] arrayName = new type[arraySize];
```

This translated into actual Java code is listed below:

```
int[]oddNumbers = new int[5];
```

The difference between this syntax and the previous one is that in this example the size of the array was created which is equal to five. In the previous example, the values of the array were inserted into it during declaration. To make more sense of arrays we need to get familiar with its terminology.

Indexes and elements

An array is an object that holds data, and in order to access that data we need two things which are the array name and the index. The **array name** is the name it was assigned when declared. As for the index, let's think of search engines. When you search in Google for some content what happens is that it returns an index of web pages. The pages are numbered 1-10 and once you click on the link you are redirected to its URL. The pages are stored in an index in Google and the values of the index are the web pages themselves. A similar process happens when data is stored in an array.

Let's take a look at the following code snippet:

```
int[]oddNumbers = {1,3,5,7,9,11};
```

The numbers in the array of ints are indexed as well. However, instead of starting from 1-10 like Google, it starts at 0 and goes to its length minus one which is nine. The values inside an array are known as its elements. In order to obtain the **elements** in an array you must use the following syntax:

```
arrayName[indexNumber];
```

Therefore, if we want to access the first element in oddNumbers, or 1, then the expression we must create is: offNumbers[0].This expression can be stored inside an integer to create a statement because an integer has the same type as the value. Therefore, the following syntax is legal:

```
int firstValue = oddNumbers[0];
```

The syntax that's used to access the elements in an array is also known as subscript notation.

Boundaries

It's important to know the boundaries of array indexes as going outside of them will generate errors. For example, as mentioned previously arrays start at index 0, and go up to its length - 1. Java provides a built in attribute for arrays known as the length property which provides the number of elements inside an array as an integer. The syntax for using it is listed below:

```
arrayName.length;
```

An example translated into Java is listed below:

```
long[] bigNums = new long[100000];

System.out.println(bigNums.length);
```

The output is: 100000

Therefore, the boundary for accessible indexes for bigNums is from 0-99999. Remember, arrays in Java start at 0, therefore the maximum index of an array will always be one less than the number of elements in an array. It's illegal to access an index that's greater than the maximum array index. Going under or over an array's boundaries will cause an ArrayIndexOutOfBoundsException. These types of errors will compile correctly but will show up when the program is run.

An illustration of the array data structure in Java is listed below:

Figure 7.2: Array data structure illustration.

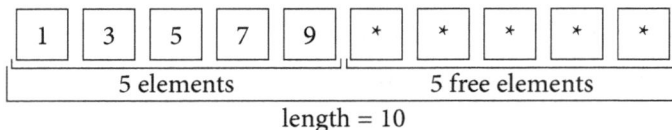

```
1   3   5   7   9   *   *   *   *   *
```

| 5 elements | 5 free elements |

length = 10

An example of code that will generate such an error is listed below:

```
byte[] offsets = {1,2,3};

byte a = offsets[3];

byte b = offsets[-1];
```

Alternative array formats

It's typical to see arrays declared with this syntax:

```
arrayType[] arrayName;
```

However, even though its convention that's not the only way to declare an array in Java. Instead of putting the square brackets ([]) directly behind the type of array, you can also put the square brackets outside of the name of the array. Therefore, the following syntax is legal in Java:

```
arrayType arrayName[];
```

However, this format is typically frowned upon by the developer community due to being more difficult to read. In some language like C++ for example, arrays are typically declared behind the name of the array. Java ensures compatibility for developers who have a penchant for putting the square brackets after the array name.

In addition, there's another way that you can format arrays. If you declare and initialize your array, then Java permits you to use what's known as the shortcut syntax listed below:

```
int []compositeNumbers = {
                4,   6,   8,   9,
                10, 12, 14, 15,
                16, 18, 20, 21
        };
```

Iterating over arrays

There are two ways to iterate over arrays: old-fashioned and new-fashion. The old-fashioned method is to use a `for` loop. The syntax is listed below:

```
for( int i = 0; i < arrayName.length; i++) {
                System.out.println(arrayName[i]);
        }
```

What this does is set the counter equal to 0 and then iterate all the way up to one less than the array length. It prints out all the values of the array by accessing the changing indexes in the array.

An example of this in Java is listed below:

Figure 7.3: Array iteration example.

```
double[] decimalPoints = new double[5];
        decimalPoints[0] = 2.0;
```

```
decimalPoints[1] = 0.27;

decimalPoints[2] = 17.7;

decimalPoints[3] = 9.22;

decimalPoints[4] = 99.2;

for(int i = 0; i < decimalPoints.length; i++) {

    System.out.print(decimalPoints[i] + " ");

}
```

The output is: 2.0 0.27 17.7 9.22 99.2

However, something known as the enhanced for loop was introduced in Java 5 which makes iterating over arrays easier.

The syntax for using the enhanced for loop is listed below:

```
for( type newArray: oldArray) {

// statements

}
```

The syntax translated into Java code is listed below:

Figure 7.4: Enhanced for loop demo.

```
String[] names = {"Dan", "Alex", "Carlos", "Deshaun"};

    for(String printNames : names)

        System.out.print(printNames + " ");
```

Enhanced for loops are a nice addition that you should add to your programming repertoire, but it does have its drawbacks. For example, if you want to access an element of an array within an enhanced for loop you won't be able to do that.

Manipulating elements in an array

When arrays are created they're of a certain type, and those type's operations can be performed on the elements of an array.

For example, let's create an array of Strings that contain lower case vowels of a, e, i, o, and u. If we want to convert the lowercase characters into uppercase ones then we could use the toUpperCase() method from the String class on the individual elements of the array. For example, look at the following code snippet:

Figure 7.5: Manipulating elements of an array example.

```
String[] lowerCaseVowels = { "a", "e", "i", "o", "u" };

    for(int i = 0;i<lowerCaseVowels.length;i++)

    {

        lowerCaseVowels[i] = lowerCaseVowels[i].
        toUpperCase();

        System.out.print(lowerCaseVowels[i] + " ");

    }
```

The output is: A E I O U

Let's try another example to gain more experience with manipulating the values inside elements of an array. Let's imagine that we have the daily sales of a computer store in an array format:

```
double[] todaySales = {489.1, 262.99, 99.981, 567.99};
```

How would we compute the total sales of the store? One solution is to iterate over every element of the array and then the sum that element with a placeholder variable. The code for this is written below:

```
double sales = 0.0;

    for(int i = 0;i<todaySales.length;i++) {

        sales += todaySales[i];

    }

    System.out.println("Total sales for today is
    "+sales);
```

The output is: Total sales for today is 1420.0610000000001

Passing arrays to constructors

Arrays like primitive and reference types can be passed as parameters to constructors and methods. If you want to pass an array as an argument to a constructor then there must first be a constructor in the class which accepts arrays as arguments. You can then create the local variable within the main method, instantiate the class, and then pass the array name as an argument to the constructor. The following code illustrates this process. The code is within the main method.

```
int[] firstTen = {0,1,2,3,4,5,6,7,8,9};

NaturalNumbers nums1 = new NaturalNumbers(firstTen);

NaturalNumbers nums2 = new NaturalNumbers(new int[5]);
```

Note, arrays can also be passed without a name using the expression new int[dimension]. However, it must specify its dimensions or less a compile error will generate.

Passing arrays to methods

The process of passing arrays to methods is similar to that of constructors. You must create an object, and then use that object to invoke the method which will be the name of a local array you created. The following code snippet shows a method that doubles the elements of the array passed to it.

Figure 7.6: Passing arrays into a method.

```
public class PassingArrays {

    public void doubleElements(int[] arrayName) {

        for (int i = 0; i < arrayName.length; i++) {

            arrayName[i] *= 2;

            System.out.print(arrayName[i] + " ");

        }

    }

    public static void main(String[] args) {

        int[] firstTen = { 0, 1, 2, 3, 4, 5, 6, 7, 8,
        9 };

        PassingArrays nums = new PassingArrays();

        nums.doubleElements(firstTen);

    }

}
```

Passing an array to the main method

It's time to revisit the very first chapter in this book which introduced the seemingly ubiquitous main method in Java which is `public static void main(String [ ] args)`. At this point we should now be able to make sense of this code. What's happening is that it declares a static method named main that has a return type of `void`. Inside of the method is an array of Strings named `args`. We can pass Strings directly to the main method by using the name of the array which is `args` along with its subscripts. We can then type in the arguments we want to pass by entering the command java argument$_1$...argument$_2$...argument$_n$. For example, the following code prints the first two arguments that are passed into the main method.

```
public static void main(String [] args) {

System.out.println(args[0] + " " + args[1]);

}
```

After compiling the code type in two Strings after the run command like in the following example: `java NaturalNumbers hey there`

The text that will be printed to the command prompt is: `hey there`

Copying arrays

If an array is created and initialized then its size is fixed and therefore cannot be changed. For example, the following code will produce a compile error:

```
int[] ofThrees = {3, 6, 9, 12};

ofThrees = {3, 6, 9};
```

If you need to create arrays that are dynamic then it's recommended to look at ArrayLists which you'll learn in chapter 8. However, into the meantime let's learn some workarounds with arrays. If you want to change the size of an array then one solution is to create a second array, and then input all of the elements of the first array into the second one. The process is shown in the following code snippet:

Figure 7.7: Copying arrays.

```
public class CopyingArrays {

    public static void main(String[] args) {

        int[] oldArray = { 1, 1, 2, 2, 3, 3, 4, 4 };

        int[] newArray = new int[16]; // doubles the
        size
```

```
for (int i = 0; i < oldArray.length; i++) {

    newArray[i] += oldArray[i];

    System.out.print(newArray[i] + " ");

}

}

}
```

The output is: 1 1 2 2 3 3 4 4

In addition to the elements from the old array being copied into the new one, the new array also has 8 more uninitialized elements. The array class also has a copyOf( ) method which will be explained in the "A Tour of the Array Class" section.

Multidimensional arrays

The arrays that we fiddled with thus far are one dimensional arrays. Java enables arrays to be made of multi dimensions which are declared and accessed slightly different. Multidimensional arrays are useful when you want to arrange values in a table format, for example rows and columns.

Below is the syntax for declaring a multidimensional array in Java:

```
type[][] = new type[size][size];
```

The following code creates a multidimensional array that has five rows and four columns with twenty elements total:

```
int[][] table = new int[5][4];
```

To iterate over multidimensional arrays you'll need to use nested loops. For example, the following code creates a 5 x 4 multidimensional array, and then prints out its default values which are 0s:

Figure 7.8: Iterating over multidimensional arrays.

```
public class MultiDimensionalArrays {

    public static void main(String[] args) {

        int[][] table = new int[5][4];

        for (int i = 0; i < 5; i++) {

            for (int j = 0; j < 4; j++) {
```

```
                    System.out.print(table[i][j]   +   "
                    ");
            }
            System.out.println();
        }
    }
}
```

The output is as follows:

0 0 0 0

0 0 0 0

0 0 0 0

0 0 0 0

0 0 0 0

Like one-dimensional arrays you can create multidimensional array literals. An example is listed below:

Figure 7.9: Multidimensional array literals.

```
int[][] sumsofFives = { {05, 10, 15, 20, 25},
                        {30, 35, 40, 45, 50},
                        {55, 60, 65, 70, 75},
                        {80, 85, 90, 95, 100},
                      };

System.out.println(sumsofFives[0][1] + sumsofFives[2][2]);
```

The output is: 75.

The element at [0][1] is 10, and the element at [2][2] is 65, summed together equals 75.

A tour of the array class

The array class hosts a suite of methods for manipulating arrays. In this section we'll get acquainted with some of the more popular ones. Note, when you use methods from the array class you should import the class which is: `java.util.Arrays.`

binarySearch()

This method searches an array for a specific value and then returns the key, or the index of where the value is located. There are 18 overrides for this method. The version of the binarySearch() method that we'll test has the following details:

```
static binarySearch(int[]a, int key)
```

The below code snippet shows the method in action:

```
int[] nums = {1, 3, 5, 7, 9, 11};

int key = Arrays.binarySearch(nums, 7);

System.out.println(key);
```

The output is: 3

The output is: 3

copyOf()

This method takes a copy of an array and then returns the copy. This method has 10 overrides. The version of the method we'll test is listed below:

```
static char[] copyOf(char[] original, int newLength)
```

An example of the method in action is listed below:

```
char[] vowels = {'a','e','i','o','u'};

char[] newVowels = Arrays.copyOf(vowels,5);

    for(char content : newVowels)

    System.out.print(content + " ");
```

The output is: a e i o u

equals()

As the name suggests it compares the content of two arrays to determine if they're equal. The method has nine overrides. The version of the equals() method that we'll implement is listed below:

```
double emptyLot[] = new double[5];

double[] emptyDoubles = new double[5];
```

```
boolean truth = Arrays.equals(emptyLot,emptyDoubles);

System.out.println(truth);
```

The output is: true.

fill()

This method fills the index of arrays with specified values. This method has 18 overrides. The details for the version of `fill()` that we'll implement is listed below:

```
fill(long[]a, long val)
```

An example of the method in action is listed in the following code snippet:

```
long numbers[] = new long[5];

Arrays.fill(numbers, 262726627);

    for(long nums: numbers)

    System.out.print(nums + " ");
```

The output is: 262726627 262726627 262726627 262726627 262726627

sort()

This method shorts an array in ascending order (least to greatest). This method has 18 overrides. The version of the method I'm going to implement is listed below:

```
sort(int[] a)
```

Below is the `sort()` method in action.

```
int[]listOfItems = {22, 73, 191, 93, 1082, 37, 747, 232, 484, 8686, 2, 27, 58};

Arrays.sort(listOfItems);

for(int items : listOfItems)

    System.out.print(items + " ");
```

The output is: 2 22 27 37 58 73 93 191 232 484 747 1082 8686

toString()

The `toString()` method converts an array into a String. The method has 9 overrides. Below is the version of the method that we'll use:

`static String toString(float[ ]a)`

Here's the `toString()` method in action:

`float[ ] temperatures = {85.8f,75.3f,79.90f};`

`String results = Arrays.toString(temperatures);`

`System.out.println(results);`

The output is: `[85.8, 75.3, 79.9]`

Chapter 7 Re-factored

In this chapter you learned the basics for creating and manipulating arrays in Java. Arrays are special objects that enable the storage of multiple values. Arrays are found in a variety of programming languages, and its popularity is due to the fact that arrays are incredibly efficient in storing and accessing objects. You would want to use an array to hold many objects of an equal type. Arrays can be iterated, searched, sorted, compared, and computed.

Chapter 7 Resources

Array Classes: https://docs.oracle.com/javase/8/docs/api/java/util/Arrays.html

Chapter 7 Exercises

1) T or F: An array is a special kind of object.

2) T or F: An array can only hold primitive types.

3) T or F: The values of an array are called its members.

4) T or F: Arrays may consist of one or more types.

5) T or F: Arrays are indexed starting a zero.

6) T or F: The valid indexes of an array range from 0 to n-1, where n represents the length of the array.

7) T or F: Once an array is created its length can never be changed.

8) T or F: Square brackets ([]) are needed when creating arrays.

9) T or F: The square brackets must come after the type of an array.

10) T or F: Array instances are objects. Therefore, they inherit the methods of `java.lang.Object`.

11) T or F: when you create an array with the new keyword and specify its size, the default values of the elements will be that of the array's type.

12) T or F: An array element has a name.

13) T or F: Array declarations have constructors.

14) Change "T or F: The expression for accessing an element in an array is listed below:

```
arrayName[index];
```

15) Refer to the snippet of code for the following question:

```
String[] options = {"Yes","No","Maybeso"};
```

Write the print statements to print out *Yes* and *Maybeso*.

16) Refer to the following code snippet for this question.

```
double[] yearlySalaries = { 34_3537.37, 76_362.98,
100_827.98, 45_62827, 76_373.9383, 54_726.001,
65_2727.02828 };
```

Write code that computes the average of the elements in this array.

17) Refer to the following code snippet for this question.

```
int element = 2;
int[]numbers = {13,51,125,500,701,291};
int result = numbers[0]++ * numbers[++element];
System.out.println(result);
```

What's printed?

Chapter 7 Answers

1) True. It's an object that can hold primitive or reference types.

2) False. It can also hold reference types.

3) False. It's called elements.

4) False. It can only consist of one type.

5) True. Since arrays start at zero you can access the first element of the array by using the syntax `arrayName[0]`.

6) True. If you try to access an element of an array that's less than 0 or greater than n-1 then an `ArrayIndexOutOfBoundsException` will occur.

7) True. Once an array is created its length is fixed. If you need to copy of the elements of the array then you can use the `copyOf()` method. In addition, you can also use ArrayList if you need to create arrays that are dynamic in nature.

8) True. An array cannot be created without the square brackets.

9) False. Even though by convention the square brackets come after the type of the array, the code will still compile if the bracket comes after the name of the array.

10) True. Since arrays are objects they inherit all of the methods that are in `java.lang.Object`.

11) True. For example, if you create an array of doubles of size 50 without specifying the values of the elements, then the default values of the 50 elements will be 0.0.

12) False. The difference between an array element and a variable is that an array element doesn't have a name.

13) False. Arrays use the new keyword to construct an array object but they don't use any parenthesis which represents a call to the constructor.

14) True. This is how the elements of an array are accessed. It's also known as a subscript expression.

15) `System.out.println(options[0]);`

   `System.out.println(options[2]);`

16) `double average = 0;`

   `for (int i = 0; i < yearlySalaries.length; i++) {`

   `   average += yearlySalaries[i];`

   `}`

   `average = average / yearlySalaries.length;`

   `System.out.println(average);`

17) Output: 6500. The expression of `numbers[0]++ *`
   `numbers[++element]` is equivalent to 500 * 13 which equals 6500.

Chapter 8: Collections and Generics

A collection is something that many humans typically form at one point in life. For example, a child may collect baseball trading cards, or a music aficionado may collect old vinyl records. Even programming languages like Java have their own collections. The Java Collection framework (JCF) consists of classes and interfaces that implement reusable data structures. We'll tour the two main interfaces in this framework along with some of the commonly used classes.

The Collection Interface

There are many components to the JCF so let's start off by analyzing the hierarchy of files in this package. Having a strong understanding of this concept will help you understand the relationships between various interfaces and classes. Java partitions the Collection interfaces into two trees: The one we'll focus on now is what's considered the root interface which is: `java.util.Collection`.

The Collection interface contains the basic functionality such as `add()`, `remove()`, and `size()`. The Collection interface has three sub interfaces of `List`, `Set`, and `Queue` that provides more specialization. A `Set` doesn't contain duplicates, a `List` is ordered, and a `Queue` allows additional insertion and removal operations.

Below is a diagram that illustrates the hierarchy of the Collection class.

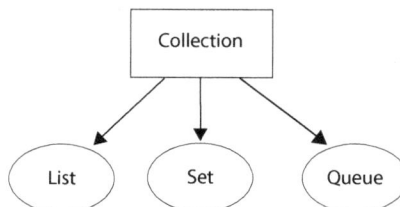

As you can see the List, Set, and Queue interfaces subclasses it.

The List interface has two super interfaces and 10 classes. Some of the List's concrete classes are ArrayList, LinkedList, Vector, and Stack.

Below is an illustration that shows the updated hierarchy:

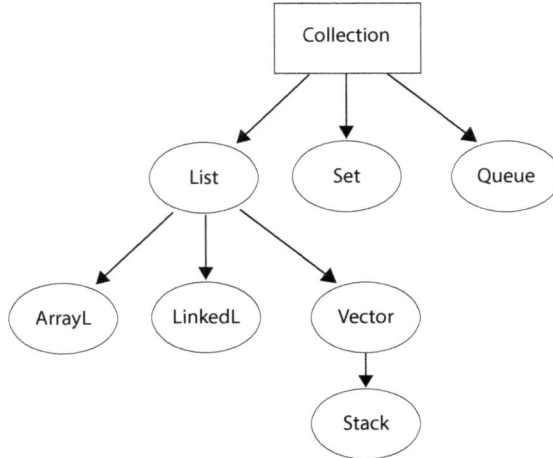

For brevity ArrayList is shortened to ArrayL, and LinkedList is shortened to LinkedL.

The Set interface has two sub interfaces and eight subclasses. The two sub interfaces of NavigableSet and SortedSet are included in the updated diagram below:

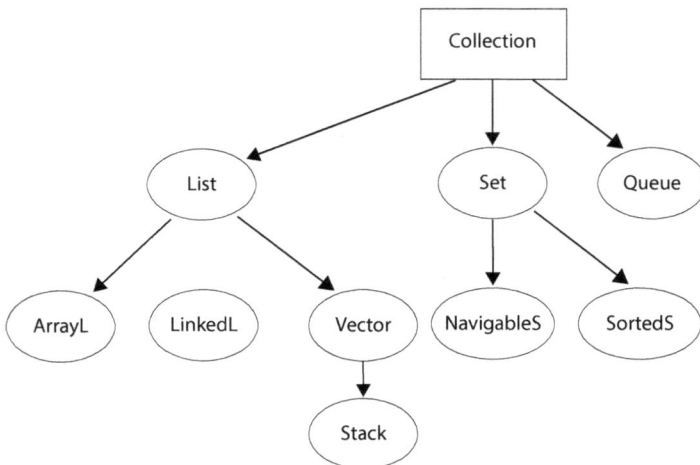

For brevity `NavigableSet` is shortened to `NavigableS`, and `SortedSet` is shortened to `SortedS`.

The `Queue` Collection is designed to hold elements prior to its processing. The Queue interface in Java has four sub interfaces and thirteen known implementing classes. Two of its sub interfaces of `Deque` and `TransferQueue` are included in the updated diagram below:

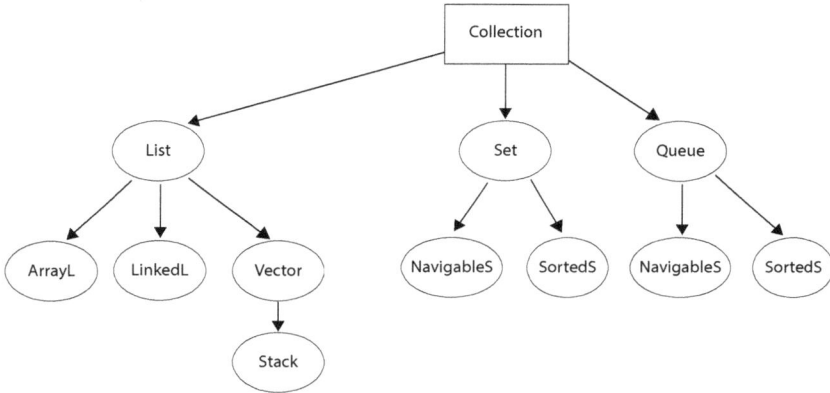

For brevity `TransferQueue` is shortened to *TransferQ*. Let's analyze some of the concrete classes of the List interface.

List Interface

The List interface is a sub interface of Collection, and represents a group of ordered objects that can be accessed in a specific order. Objects of the List interface can also be accessed by an index similar to the way an array can. Remember, interfaces can't themselves be instantiated but instead define a common set of methods that it subclasses must implement. In addition, even though an interface can't be instantiated, it can be used to instantiate a subclass that implements it. The concrete classes of the `List` interface or the ones that provide implementations of the abstract methods that we'll cover are `ArrayList`, `LinkedList`, `Vector`, and `Stack`.

ArrayList

An ArrayList is a type of List that supports dynamic or growable arrays. Remember, arrays are static meaning that once they're defined they can't grow. However, this is not the case with an ArrayList. While an ArrayList can be defined with an initial certain size, once it reaches its limit it can resize and automatically grow. It implements all of the methods in the List interface and also includes its own methods for manipulating the array size.

How to create an ArrayList

There are three constructors for the ArrayList class and 31 methods. In order to create an ArrayList you can import the entire package of where its located which is `java.util,` or you can import its individual class as indicated in the snippets of code below.

```
import java.util.*;
```

```
import java.util.ArrayList;
```

The first way to create an ArrayList is to use the following syntax:

```
ArrayList()
```

What this does is create an initial ArrayList with a size of 10. An example of the constructor in Java code is listed below:

```
ArrayList computerVirus = new ArrayList();
```

The second way to create an ArrayList constructor is listed below:

```
ArrayList(int initialCapacity)
```

An example of this in Java code is written below.

```
List music = new ArrayList(1000);
```

Remember, since ArrayList implements the List interface you can use the List class to instantiate an ArrayList. In this example the initial size of the ArrayList is 1000. To import the individual List class use the following syntax:

```
import java.util.List;
```

The third way to create an ArrayList constructor is listed below:

```
ArrayList(Collection<? extends E> c)
```

An example of this written in Java is listed below:

```
Collection<String> records = new ArrayList<String>();
```

If this is your first time seeing this notation then it may throw you off tangent. Before we dig further, we need to learn about a concept called Generics.

Intro to Generics

The class declaration of an ArrayList in the Java API states the following:

```
public class ArrayList<E>
```

You're probably wondering what's up with the diamond bracket (< >) with the E inside it. This is a concept in Generics known as **type-parameter,** which enables types like classes or interfaces to be parameters when defining a class. Just think of the concept of using parameters in your methods which allows the same code to be re-used with different input. The difference between parameters in methods and type parameters is that methods use values as arguments while type parameters uses types.

Let's create our own generic class using a type parameter listed in the code below:

```
public class CD <T> {}
```

As you can see the class declaration looks normal with the exception of the diamond bracket in which we explained previously as being a type parameter. It's convention to make type parameters single uppercase letters. The reason for this is to distinguish them from ordinary class or interface names. The commonly used type parameter names are listed below:

- E – Element (you'll use this often in the Collections framework)

- K – Key

- N – Number

- T– Type

- V – Value

- S, U, V, Z – 2nd, third, fourth, and nth types

So we created a generic class and specified the type parameter, so what's the next step? Let's invoke the generic class type by replacing T with a concrete reference type as indicated in the code snippet below:

```
public class CD <T> {
 CD <String> cdName = new CD <String>();

}
```

As you can see that when a generic type invocation was done, the T was replaced with a reference type which is a String in this case. The diamond bracket should follow the class name or less an unchecked or unsafe operation warning occur. One of the most important benefits of Generics are stronger type checking--the java compiler provides strong type checking during compilation and will issue warnings if the code violates type safety.

A Demo of an ArrayList

Some of the commonly used methods of the ArrayList class are add(), get(), and isEmpty() which are common method names found in various classes of the Java API.

Let's create an ArrayList of superheroes. The code to do this is listed below:

Figure 8.0: ArrayList creation demo.

```
import java.util.ArrayList;

public class SuperHeroes {

    public static void main(String[] args) {

        ArrayList<String> superHero = new
        ArrayList<String>();

    }

}
```

Now that the ArrayList is created let's add some superheroes to it. We can input elements into an ArrayList by using the add() method. Here's the updated code snippet below:

Figure 8.1: Adding elements to an ArrayList.

```
import java.util.ArrayList;

public class SuperHeroes {

    public static void main(String[] args) {

        ArrayList<String> superHero = new
        ArrayList<String>();

        superHero.add("Superman");

        superHero.add("Batman");

        superHero.add("Spider-Man");

        superHero.add("Hal Jordan");

        superHero.add("Wonder Woman");

        superHero.add("Martian Manhunter");

    }

}
```

Now that we have added some elements to the ArrayList we may want to retrieve some of them. ArrayLists like arrays start at index 0 but in order to retrieve items the get() method must be used. For example, the following code gets the first element we added to the ArrayList.

Figure 8.2: Retrieving items from an ArrayList.

```
String firstHero = superHero.get(0);

System.out.println(firstHero);
```

The result that's printed is: `Superman`

If we want to check that an ArrayList is empty we can use the `isEmpty()` method of the ArrayList class. The method returns `true` if the list is empty and `false` otherwise. The method in action is shown below:

```
System.out.println(superHero.isEmpty());
```

The output is `false`.

If we want to traverse the entire ArrayList and print out all of the elements in it then we can choose any of the three main options for iterating over a Collection. We'll explore them in the following section.

The classic for loop

Collections can be iterated over with the use of a traditional loop. The syntax for this is listed below:

```
for (int i = 0; i < Collection.size(); i++) {

  type variableName = Collection.get(i);

}
```

The Collection interface contains a method called `size()` which returns an int that contains the size of the Collection. This method is similar to the length attribute used in arrays to access the size of it.

A java implementation of this loop in action is listed below:

Figure 8.3: Iterating over an ArrayList–traditional loop.

```
for (int i = 0; i < superHero.size(); i++) {

  String result = superHero.get(i);
```

```
System.out.println(result);

}
```

This loop is beneficial if you also need to access the indexes of the elements. The second way to traverse a Collection is to use what's known as an Iterator.

Iterator

Interator is an Interface in Java that contains methods for iterating over a Collection. The three main methods in this class are `hasNext()`, `next()`, and `remove()`. To use the Iterator interface you must import its class which can be done by using the following code:

```
import java.util.Iterator;
```

Next, create a reference variable of type Iterator and then set it equal to the Collection that you want to traverse. Here's how it's done:

```
Iterator iteratorName = referenceVariable.iterator();
```

This translated into java code is shown below:

```
Iterator scan = superHero.iterator();
```

Iterator is an interface and therefore it can't be instantiated. The syntax for traversing a Collection with an Iterator is listed below:

```
Iterator <Type> iteratorName = referenceVariable.
iterator();

while (iteratorName.hasNext()) {

  type variableName = iteratorName.next();

}
```

This syntax translated into Java is listed below:

Figure 8.4: Iterating over an ArrayList–Iterator interface.

```
Iterator <String> scan = superHero.iterator();

while (scan.hasNext()) {

  String list = scan.next();

  System.out.println(list);

}
```

This style of iteration is beneficial if you don't need the index but you might want to remove elements in the Collection.

Enhanced for Loop

The third style for iterating over a Collection is to use the enhanced for loop. The syntax for this is shown below:

```
for(Type t : referenceVariable) {
// statements
}
```

The syntax translated into Java code is listed below:

Figure 8.5: Iterating over an ArrayList–enhanced for loop.

```
for(String s : superHero) {
System.out.println(s);
}
```

This style of iterating over a Collection is the most succinct and allows you to traverse the Collection unconditionally.

When to use an ArrayList

There are a couple of things to keep in mind when deciding to use an ArrayList in your program. The ArrayList uses an array as its underlining data structure, but compared to arrays it has the ability to dynamically re-size. Below is a summary of the Big-O notation of some of the operations in the ArrayList class.

Figure 8.6: Costs for ArrayList operations.

```
get  add  next iterator.remove
O(1) O(1) O(1) O(n)
```

If you're not familiar with **Big-O notation** then know that it's a mathematical notation for describing the limiting behavior of a function. In mathematics, a function is similar to a method in Java.

Big-O notation is concerned with analyzing a function as it trends towards a specific value or infinity. Since an ArrayList uses an array as its underlining data structure, the `get()` method or getting the index of an element is relatively cheap which is why its O(1). This is known as constant time and means that there exists a constant such that the number of operations is bounded by it.

Wrapper Classes

There will be times when we're dealing with Collections in which we will need to manipulate primitive types like an `int` or `double`. The workaround for this is to use what's known as Wrapper classes. As the name suggest these classes *wraps* around a primitive which allows it to be used as an object. Wrapper classes also have methods that unwraps the object and reveal its inwards which consist of primitive types. This process is analogous to how an envelope encases the content of a letter.

Below is the listing of 8 primitive types in Java with their associated wrapper classes which is located inside the `java.lang` package. This allows developers to use objects in the place of primitives. Remember, primitives and references are two different data types so they can't directly manipulate each other.

Figure 8.7: Table of primitive types and associated Wrapper classes.

byte	Byte
short	Short
int	Integer
long	Long
float	Float
double	Double
char	Character
boolean	Boolean

The numeric classes of `Byte, Short, Integer, Long, Float,` and `Double` are subclasses of the abstract class `Number`.

To gain a better understanding of Wrapper classes lets work with some Java code.

Let's assume that I wanted to create an ArrayList of Integers that holds even numbers from 1-20. One way to do this is as follows:

```
ArrayList <Integer> evens = new ArrayList <Integer>();
    for(int i = 1;i<=20;i++) {
        if (i % 2 == 0) {
            evens.add(i);
```

```
        }

    }
```

System.out.println(evens);The output is: `[2, 4, 6, 8, 10, 12, 14, 16, 18, 20]`

However, the code adds an `int` into the ArrayList of Integer objects. How come the Java compiler didn't generate an error? The reason for this is due to a concept called autoboxing. When the int was added to the ArrayList the compiler automatically converts i into type `Integer`. In addition, the reverse can also happen. Look at the following code snippet:

```
Integer num = new Integer(3);

int triple = num * 3;
```

This is made possible due to unboxing as the corresponding primitive type is stored in the variable `triple`.

parse()

All of the wrapper classes comes with their version of the `parse()` method. This is a static method that accepts a String argument and then converts it to its associated primitive type. For example, let's assume that you have a String like the example listed below:

```
String s = "123";
```

Even though this looks like an integer it's still a String. However, if we pass it through the `parseInt()` method of the Integer class then it converts the String into an integer as in the following example:

```
String s = "123";

int t = Integer.parseInt(s);

System.out.println(t + 5);
```

The following prints the integer 128 instead of the String 1235. If you want to convert a String into an `int` using the `parseInt()` method, then the String can oddly enough only contain integers or less a runtime error will occur. For example the following code will compile but generate a runtime error:

```
String s = "123hi";

int t = Integer.parseInt(s);
```

```
System.out.println(t + 5);
```

We can also pass in arguments into the main method, convert it to a primitive, and then perform calculations on it. The following code passes two integers to `args` and then adds them.

```
int one = Integer.parseInt(args[0]);

int two = Integer.parseInt(args[1]);

System.out.println(args[0] + " + " + args[1] + " = " +
(one + two));
```

If the arguments of 56 and 7 are passed when the code is run then the output would be 56 + 7 = 63.

LinkedList

In computer science a linked list is a simple and versatile data structure. It's composed of nodes which contains data and a pointer (link) to the next node in the sequence. There are two primary forms of LinkedLists which are singly linked lists and doubly linked lists.

The underlining data structure for a LinkedList in Java is a doubly-linked list which is illustrated below:

Figure 8.8: Doubly LinkedList illustration.

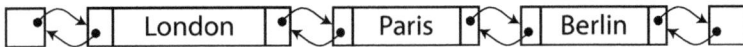

In this section we'll analyze the popular implementation of the List interface in the Java api. We'll learn how to create a LinkedList, a demo of some of its functionality, and suggested cases on when to use them.

How to create a LinkedList

To create a LinkedList you first need to import its class and then invoke one of its constructors.

To import a LinkedList class use the following code snippet: `import java.util.LinkedList;`

To construct a LinkedList use the following syntax:

```
LinkedList link = new LinkedList();
```

Unlike ArrayLists you cannot set the initial capacity of a LinkedList. The reason for this is because a LinkedList doesn't allocate memory to objects before they're added to the list. Since each node in a LinkedList holds a pointer to the next node in the list, it wouldn't be helpful to allocate memory beforehand.

Like an ArrayList a LinkedList can have parameterized types. For example, the following constructor is permissible:

```
LinkedList<String>travelRoute=newLinkedList<String>();
```

A Demo of a LinkedList

The LinkedList class has two constructors and 39 methods. Let's create a LinkedList that lists some of the cities of Europe. We first must import the LinkedList class, and then invoke a constructor. After that's done we can use the add( ) method to insert an object into the LinkedList as indicated in the code snippet below:

Figure 8.9: Creating a LinkedList and adding items.

```
import java.util.LinkedList;

public class LinkedListDemo {

    public static void main(String[] args) {

        LinkedList<String>   europeanCities   =   new
        LinkedList<String>();

        europeanCities.add("Paris");

        europeanCities.add("London");

        europeanCities.add("Lisbon");

        europeanCities.add("Amsterdam");

        europeanCities.add("Berlin");

    }

}
```

The LinkedList class have an addFirst( ) and addLast( ) method which is not found in the ArrayList class. At the name suggests these methods allow you to insert an element into the front or back of the LinkedList. The below code snippet shows you how to do this:

```
europeanCities.addFirst("Madrid");
```

```
europeanCities.addLast("Rotterdam");
```

If you need to retrieve the first and last elements in the list then you can use the getFirst() and getLast() methods.

Below is the code snippet on how to retrieve these items:

```
String first = europeanCities.getFirst();

String last = europeanCities.getLast();
```

The LinkedList class also provides a method called indexOf() that allows you to retrieve an object in a list based on the index number you enter. Below is the code on how to retrieve the first occurrence of an element in a list.

```
int lastIndex = europeanCities.indexOf("Paris");
```

The result when printed is: 0.

The ways for iterating over a Collection applies to a LinkedList since the LinkedList class implements the Link interface which in turn extends Collection. The following code traverses the LinkedList and then prints out its elements:

Figure 8.10: Traversing a LinkedList.

```
for (String s: europeanCities)

    System.out.print(s + " ");
```

The output is: Madrid Paris London Lisbon Amsterdam Berlin Rotterdam

When to use a LinkedList

Some real world examples of where LinkedLists are used is in the FAT file system which uses them as its directory structure, and bash which uses them to store arguments in a program. LinkedLists should be considered if you're unsure of how many items will be in the list, and if you want to add or remove elements from the beginning or the end of the list as this will be constant time or O(1). If you need to insert or remove items from the middle of the list then this can be expensive with the worst case scenario being O(n).

Stack

Let's learn a little history about Java. The early version of Java didn't have the Collections framework, as Collections was released in version 1.2. Prior to Collections there were several classes and one interface to store objects. When the Collection interface came along these older classes were updated to be compatible with Collections. Since these classes were around from the beginning of Java they're sometimes referred to as *legacy classes*. The legacy classes are `Dictionary, Vector, Hashtable, Properties,` and `Stack`. They're not deprecated yet but they're rarely used now. However, one of the legacy classes that we'll analyze is `Stacks` since they're important data structures in computer science.

Before we learn about the `Stack` class in Java lets first understand one thing. There's a difference between an abstract data structure, and its concrete implementation. A stack can be defined as an abstract data type which acts as a container for objects. Stacks have two explicit features which are to push (add) data, and pop (remove) data. Stacks are a Last in First Out type of data structure, or *LIFO* for short. To remember that stack is a *LIFO* data structure just think of the concept of stacking everyday objects. For example, if you were to stack 50 pieces of paper in the binder then the first piece of paper that you remove will be the last one you just put in adhering to the concept of last-in first-out.

The concept of a Stack can also be thought of when someone stacks trays or plates in a cafeteria. The last tray to be added to the pile will be the first one out. The JVM stack is a portion of memory that contains the methods, local variables, and reference variables––reference variables can also be inside a heap if an object holds a reference variable.

A Demo of the Stack Class

The Stack class has one constructor and five methods. It implements 6 interfaces which are `Serializable, Cloneable, Iterable, Collection, List,` and `RandomAccess`. The `Stack` class also extends the `Vector` class and is therefore a subset of it.

To create a Stack in Java you can import its class and then create a Stack constructor. To import the individual Stack class use this snippet of code: `import java.util.Stack;`

To construct a Stack object use the following syntax: `Stack<Type>books = new Stack<Type>();`

When a Stack is created it contains no items. Trying to pass a value into a Stack will lead to a compile error. Below are the methods in the Stack class: `push(), pop(), peek(), empty(),` and `search()`.

One mnemonic device to remember three of the methods in the class is the *three p's*: push, pop, and peek. The `push()` method adds an item to the top of the stack.

The details for this method are listed below:

```
E push(E item)
```

The parameter is E *item* and it `returns` a value of type E. Remember, the letter E is just notation to label a type parameter for an element. You can create a Stack constructor without specifying its type, for example, the following will compile albeit warnings. In order to view the details of the warnings you can compile your file with the following format:

```
javac– Xlint ClassName.java
```

```
The warnings that show up are listed below:
```

```
  StackDemo.java: 9: warning: [rawtypes] found raw type:
  Stack
```

```
Stack books = new Stack(); ^
```

The compiler is warning you that your use of raw types, or non-parameterized types. To make those nasty looking warnings go away along with avoiding future runtime errors, add type parameters, and then push elements into the stack of the same type. Here's the code for that:

Figure 8.11: Pushing elements to a stack.

```
Stack<String> books = new Stack<String>();

            books.push("In Search of Lost Time");

            books.push("Ulysses");

            books.push("Don Quixote");

            books.push("Moby Dick");

            books.push("Hamlet");
```

The pop( ) method removes the item at the very top of the stack and then returns it. The specifications for the method are listed below:

```
E pop()
```

Imagine that you had books and then stack the one-by-one. The very first book that you retrieve from the stack will be the last one you just stacked, which adheres to the LIFO data structure. Therefore, what will be the result when the following code is executed?

```
String poppedBook = books.pop();
```

```
System.out.println(poppedBook);
```

The answer is `Hamlet` since it's the last book to be stacked.

The `peep()` method peeps inside the stack without removing any of the elements. The specification for the method is listed below:

```
E peek()
```

Here's the code for implementing that.

```
String peekaboo = books.peek();
```

```
System.out.println(peekaboo);
```

The String `Moby Dick` will be printed but it will remain in the stack.

When to use a Stack

Stacks are one of the simplest data structures but don't let its simplicity deceive you. It's very important and has many applications across the computing realm. For example, web browsers commonly use stacks to store the number of urls a user has accessed. Every time a web-user browse a new site, that site's url is pushed into the stack. Stacks are also commonly used in text editors to implement the undo and redo features and as evidence by the JVM implementation they're also not a bad choice for runtime memory management.

Also, since a Stack is LIFO data structure it can be used to reverse the ordering of a word through the `pop()` method. For example, let's say that we have the String Hello and want to print the order in reverse. We can create a Stack of Strings, push the letters into the stack, create an iterator to traverse the stack, and then pop the elements from it. A sample implementation is listed below:

Figure 8.12: Printing a word in reverse using a Stack.

```
Stack<String> reverse = new Stack<String>();

        reverse.push("H");

        reverse.push("e");

        reverse.push("l");

        reverse.push("l");

        reverse.push("o");

        Iterator<String> scan = reverse.iterator();
```

```
while (scan.hasNext()) {

        System.out.print(reverse.pop() + " ");

    }
```

The output is: o l l e H

Queues

The Queue is a type of Collection for holding elements prior to processing. Queues in Java typically use First in First out (FIFO) ordering which means that the first element to be added will be the first one out when a remove method is called. What makes the Queue class interesting is that it methods has two forms. One, it throws an exception if an operation fails and two, it returns a special value if it fails. Let's analyze a concrete class of the Queue interface which is PriorityQueue. According to the class the objects are ordered according to their natural ordering or via a Comparator provided during the Queue construction. A PriorityQueue does not permit null elements and its capacity automatically grows as more elements are added.

Below is a demo of the PriorityQueue class.

Figure 8.13: PriorityQueue demo.

```
import java.util.PriorityQueue;

PriorityQueue <String> list = new PriorityQueue
<String>();

list.add("Mount Kilimanjaro");

list.add("Table Mountain");

list.add("Robben Island");

list.add("Masai Mara");

list.add("Kruger National");

while (!list.isEmpty()) {

  System.out.println(list.poll())
```

The output of the following is:

```
Kruger National
```

```
Masai Mara

Mount Kilimanjaro

Robben Island

Table Mountain
```

As you can see the `poll()` method enables the natural ordering of the Objects as the results are printed in lexicographical order. A real world example in which a PriorityQueue could be considered is thread scheduling.

Sets

A set is a collection in which duplicates are not allowed. There are three general purpose Set implementations which are HashSet, TreeSet, and LinkedHashSet. Which one to use depends on the situation. The HashSet class is faster than TreeSet as it has constant time on most operations versus log-time for most TreeSet operations. However, if you need your Set to be sorted then HashSet may not be the best solution and you may want to look into TreeSet which implements the SortedSet interface and therefore maintains the order. The LinkedHashSet uses both a hashtable and a linked list and has a similar performance to a HashSet while maintaining insertion order. The reason why the ordering is maintained is because the LinkedHashSet uses a doubly linked list. Let's demo the HashSet class to gain some familiarity with the interface.

To be able to use the HashSet class you must import the class and then invoke one of its constructors.

To import the HashSet class use the following code snippet: `import java.util.HashSet;`

Let's create a HashSet object with parameterized type of String. The code for doing that is listed below:

```
HashSet<String> employee = new HashSet<String>();
```

Let's take a closer look at the HashSet class. We can see that it has four constructors and 8 methods. Like any class that implements the List interface we can use the `add()` method to input elements into it. The code for doing that is listed below:

```
employee.add("Susan J. Trimble");

employee.add("Freddie J. Rivera");

employee.add("Paul B. Ulrich");
```

```
employee.add("Srinivasa Ramanujan");
```

We can also use the enhanced for loop to iterate over the elements in the list. The code for that is listed below:

```
for(String s : employee)

  System.out.println(s + " ");
```

Now here's the interesting thing about HashSets. When you print the elements there's no guarantee that the order will remain the same. For example, here's the output of the code:

```
Susan J. Trimble

Srinivasa Ramanujan

Freddie J. Rivera

Paul B. Ulrich
```

As you can see the output doesn't maintain the same order as the way it was inserted.

Maps

Here's the lowdown on Maps. A Map object works by pairing keys to values, nd no duplicate keys are permissiable. The Map interface

is not considered a true collection because Maps function differently than a collection. If the functionality is drastically different then it wouldn't make much sense for a Map to subclass the Collection interface.

The Map interface has several classes that implement it, and the one we'll observe is HashMap. This class is similar to the hash table legacy class except that it's unsynchronized and does not allow null values. The HashMap class makes not guarantees that the ordering will remain constant.

To create a HashMap we'll need to import its class and then construct a HashMap object. The code for importing a HashMap is listed below:

```
import java.util.HashMap;
```

One way to create a HashMap object is as follows:

```
HashMap<Integer, Integer>map = new HashMap<Integer,
Integer>();
```

Since a Map specifies key value pairs two parameterized types must be passed when the constructor is created or less a compile error will occur. To add values to a HashMap you use the put(K key, V value) method. An example of it is action is represented below:

```
map.put(1,500);

map.put(0,20);
```

If you want to access a value that's mapped by a key then you'll need to use the get(Object key) method. An example of this method in action is listed below:

```
int value = map.get(1);
```

One way to iterate over a Map is to use the getKey() and getValue() methods from the Map interface. In order to use them you'll need to import the Map interface as listed here:

```
import java.util. Map;

 for (Map.Entry<Integer, Integer> print : map.entrySet()) {

        System.out.println("Get key " + print.getKey() +
        ": " + print.getValue());

 }
```

Chapter 8 Re-factored

In this chapter you got a basic introduction to the Collections framework in java. A Collection is an object that represents a group of objects that be manipulated independently of its implementation details. Some of the benefits of Collections are decreased programming effort, better performance, and software reuse.

Chapter 8 Resources

Byte class: https://docs.oracle.com/javase/8/docs/api/java/lang/Byte.html

Short class: https://docs.oracle.com/javase/8/docs/api/java/lang/Short.html

Integer class: https://docs.oracle.com/javase/8/docs/api/java/lang/Integer.html

Long class: https://docs.oracle.com/javase/8/docs/api/java/lang/Long.html

Float class: https://docs.oracle.com/javase/8/docs/api/java/lang/Float.html

Double class: https://docs.oracle.com/javase/8/docs/api/java/lang/Double.html

Character class: https://docs.oracle.com/javase/8/docs/api/java/lang/Character.html

Boolean class: https://docs.oracle.com/javase/8/docs/api/java/lang/Boolean.html

Collections: https://docs.oracle.com/javase/8/docs/api/java/util/Collection.html

Collections framework overview: https://docs.oracle.com/javase/8/docs/tech-notes/guides/collections/overview.html

Stacks: https://docs.oracle.com/javase/8/docs/api/java/util/Stack.html

Graphviz: http://www.graphviz.org (the software used to make the tree diagrams in this chapter)

Chapter 8 Questions

1. T or F: If you want to use all of the classes part of the Collections package, you must use the following statement: import java.util.*;

2. T or F: Since J2SE 5.0, the collections framework has been updated to include generics. This means that you can specify the precise type that wil be stored in a Collection.

3. T or F: A Collection can't be converted into an array.

4. T or F: A List cannot contain duplicate elements.

5. T or F: List indexed is 0-based like arrays.

6. T or F: The following snippet of code compiles without errors.

```
List car = new List();
```

7. T or F: An ArrayList is a resizable implementation of a List.

8. T or F: Linked Lists starts at index 0.

Chapter 8 Answers

1. True. You can import the classes individually such as `java.util.ArrayList`.

2. True. Generics allow you to paramterize the type of Collection of a class. For example, `List<Integer> hours` can can only contain Integer values.

3. False.

4. False. Lists can contain duplicate elements; it's a Set that cannot contain duplicate elements.

5. True. They both have an index that starts a 0.

6. False. A List is an interface and therefore can't be instantiated.

7. True. That's one of the many distinction between an ArrayList and an array, is that arrays are static while ArrayLists are dynamic.

8. False, they start at index 1.

Chapter 9: Lambdas

One of the most significant updates to Java 8 has been the inclusion of lambdas. This has been touted as a long missing feature and is similar to closures in functional programming languages like Scala. The Greek symbol λ (lambda) is used in various topics in math and science but the subject that correlates closely to lambdas in Java is lambda calculus. This branch of mathematics is different from multivariable calculus and is for expressing computation based on function abstraction and application. Lambda calculus is an important field in the study of computer programming languages and in this chapter we'll explore their benefits.

The benefits of lambdas in java

A lambda can be defined as an anonymous piece of code. Lambdas are functions, and functions are the subject we learned about in Algebra. It's a type of expression that takes in input and returns a value. Before we start learning about the basics of lambdas in Java we're going to explore the benefits of using them in the first place. Below are some of the benefits on why you should consider using lambdas in your code.

Anonymous functions: Thinking of appropriate variable names can be a time consuming task. Since lambdas allow programmers to implement anonymous functions, a name is not needed.

No need for anonymous inner classes: Lambdas operate as anonymous functions and therefore can be substituted for anonymous inner classes. A benefit for this according to Oracle is reduced overhead.

Code reuse: Lambdas can be viewed as a block of code that can be passed around. This helps make code more reusable as functions can now be passed around in a similar manner that doubles or Strings are passed into a method.

Functional interfaces

In chapter 5 we were introduced to the concepts of interfaces. For a quick recap an interface is a type that specifies the behaviors that classes must implement. An interface must contain at least one abstract method, or one that include its signature without any implementation details. Just like Java enables multiple types of classes such as `public, private, protected,` or inner, there are also various kinds of interfaces. The type of interface we'll focus on is known as a functional interface which can contain exactly one abstract method. It's possible for a functional interface to contain multiple `static` and `default` methods, but it's not possible for the functional interface to contain more than one abstract method.

An example of a popular functional interface in the Java API is the interface `Runnable`. This interface should be implemented by any class whose instances should be executed by a thread. A thread is a set of register values that controls the order of execution in programs. The `Runnable` interface has one method called `run()` which runs in a separately executing thread once an object implementing `Runnable` creates a thread. Remember, in order to instantiate an interface you must create a new class, implement the interface, and override any abstract methods.

However, a popular variation of creating and starting a thread is to create an anonymous inner class and pass it to the thread's inner constructor as indicated in the code snippet below:

Figure 9.0: A thread with anonymous inner class example.

```
public class Speed {

    public static void main(String[] args) {

        new Thread(new Runnable() {

            @Override

            public void run() {

                System.out.println("Hello from
                inside the thread");

            }

        }).start();

    }

}
```

The anonymous class allows us to take a little shortcut. We don't need to create a class that implements `Runnable`, and we can create a thread, pass in a `Runnable` instance, and run it. However, anonymous inner classes aren't exactly the most elegant thing in Java. After years of tinkering with adding functional programming to the language the Java designers figured out how to make it all fit into Java 8. The above expression can be rewritten with lambdas and will look like the following:

Figure 9.1: A thread with lambda example.

```java
class Speed {

    public static void main(String[] args) {

        Runnable go = () -> System.out.println("Hello
        from inside the thread");

        new Thread(go).run();

    }

}
```

As you can see from the above lambdas help make code more concise and readable.

Let's walk through some easy examples of Lambdas so that we'll get more comfortable with them. Let's create a functional interface called `Addition` that has the signature of an abstract method called `addNums()`. The details for it are listed below:

```java
interface Addition {

    int addNums(int num1, int num2);

}
```

Now, let's create a class called `Test`.

```java
public class Test {

    public static void main(String[] args) {

        Addition sumNumbers = (int a, int b) -> a +
        b;

        System.out.println(sumNumbers.addNums(40,
        50));

    }

}
```

The output is: 90

If we were to create a normal class that implements the interface then what we would have to implement the `addNums()` method in order for the program to compile. However, as you can see with lambdas this is not the case. Let's break down the code bit-by-bit:

```
Addition sumNumbers
```

Addition is the name of the interface and `sumNumbers` is a variable that holds the result of the expression. What's happening is that the `addNums()` method in the `Addition` interface is being implemented. This is logical because the `addSums()` method is abstract and contains just the method signature. Therefore, it's useful if the lambda provides some type of implementation instructions so that the `addSum()` method can perform an action.

```
(int a, int b)
```

The content enclosed inside the parenthesis denotes the parameters. The parameters are not needed if the abstract method in the functional interface doesn't specify any, but the empty parentheses are needed regardless. In this example there are two parameters of type int. The types in this situation are optional. Therefore, the following code snippet will compile without errors: `Addition sumNumbers = (a, b) -> a + b;`

The reason why the type is not needed is because the compiler should be able to deduce the return type based on the context of the code. For example, the summing of two integers will result in an integer and luckily for us the compiler is smart enough to figure this out.

```
->
```

This is the arrow token. If you have never seen it before then the reason being is that it was non-existent prior to Java 8. It helps partition the lambda expression and let those looking at the code know that it's a lambda. To the left of the arrow are the parameters and to the right of it is the expression.

```
a + b
```

This is the expression and can be included within a code block by using curly braces to make it more readable. Lambda expressions that span multiple lines of code are typically placed within curly braces like normal blocks of code.

The syntax behind a lambda

There are various styles that one can choose when creating their lambda expressions. Below are examples of some of the more popular ones.

```
FunctionalInterface variableName = (parameter 1,
parameter 2, …, parameter n) -> {

  //statements

}
```

This style is similar to the one we just analyzed. It has the name of the `FunctionalInterface` followed by a variable. It has parameters wrapped inside parenthesis, followed by an arrow, and then optional curly braces to enclose the content of the expression inside. A mnemonic device to remember the syntax is to refer back to functional notation. For example, look at the following:

```
f(x) = 5x + 1
```

The inputs or parameters of the function are held to the left of the equal sign, and the expression is to the right of the equal sign. The java equivalent is similar but the arrow is used instead of the equal sign. For example, here's how this will look in Java:

```
x -> 5x + 1
```

Let's take a look at another popular syntax for lambdas.

```
FunctionalInterface variableName() -> {

  //statements

}
```

This syntax is identical to the previous once except that it has no parameters. This means that functional interface it implicitly implements doesn't accept any. An example of such an interface and an associated lambda expression is listed below:

```
interface Multiply {

    void times();

}


public class LambTests {

    public static void main(String[] args) {

        Multiply result = () -> System.out.println(5
        * 5);

        result.times();

    }

}
```

@FunctionalInterface

You can annotate your lambdas by using @FunctionalInterface. This is not required and your code will still compile without errors even if you were to exclude this. However, there are some benefits for including it:

- Indicates to the compiler that an interface is intended to be a functional interface.

- Ensures that the type is an interface type and not an annotation type, enum, or class.

- Ensures that the annotated type meets the standards of a functional interface.

In layman terms the @FunctionalInterface annotation enables stronger type checking. Below is a code snippet of the annotation in action:

```
@FunctionalInterface

public interface FunctionalInterFaceDemo {

 public void executeThisBaby(int a, int b);

}
```

Recap of lambda expression elements

A lambda expression may consist of the following ingredients:

- Arrow token (->): It separates the parameter or left side from the expression or right side.

- Curly braces ({...}): You don't need to include them if the lambda body is a single expression.

- Parameters: If the function doesn't have any parameters then the parenthesis would have nothing in it.

- Return keyword: Including the return keyword is not illegal with lambdas but its overkill as the compiler will know the return type by context.

Now that we understand the various benefits of lambdas let's explore the java. util.function package and analyze some of the premade functional interfaces in it.

java.util.function package

This package in Java provides a myriad of premade functional interfaces that you can quickly use to create lambda expressions for various situations. There are over 40 interfaces in this package and we're going to explore a couple of them in order to gain familiarity with this package.

Consumer<T>

This is a functional interface that accepts an argument T and returns no result (void). Below is an example of the interface being put into action:

```java
import java.util.function.Consumer;

public class FunctionTest {

    public static void main(String[] args) {

        Consumer<Integer> consume = (a) -> System.
        out.println(Integer.MAX_VALUE);

        consume.accept(1);

    }

}
```

The output for the lambda expression is: 2147483647

Interface Supplier<T>

This interface represents a supplier of results. This interface doesn't require that a new result be returned when the supplier is invoked. This interface has one method which is get and as the name indicates it retrieves a result. Below is the interface in action:

```java
import java.util.function.Supplier;

public class FunctionTest {

    public static void main(String[] args) {

        Supplier<Double> test = () -> 15.0;

        System.out.println(test.get());

    }

}
```

The output is: 15

Interface IntToLongFunction

This interface has a function that accepts an int value argument and then produces a long value result. You can use the applyAsLong() method in order to apply the function to the argument. An example of the interface in action is listed below:
import java.util.function.IntToLongFunction;

```
import java.util.function.Supplier;

public class FunctionTest {

    public static void main(String[] args) {

        Supplier<Double> test = () -> 15.0;

        System.out.println(test.get());

    }

}
```

The output is: 9223372036854775803

BiFunction<T,U,R>

This interface represents a function that can take in two arguments and produce a result. Below are the details for its type arguments.

T – The type of the first argument

U – The type of the second argument

R- The type of the result of the function

Below is an implementation of the interface using lambdas.

```
import java.util.function.BiFunction;

public class FunctionTest {

    public static void main(String[] args) {

        BiFunction<Integer, Integer, Integer> biTest
        = (x, y) -> 2 * x + 2 * y;

        System.out.println(biTest.apply(2828, 27));

    }

}
```

The only new thing you haven't seen yet is the `apply()` function which is part of the `BiFunction` Interface. What this method does is apply the function to the given argument. Therefore, the arguments of 2828 and 27 are passed into the function respectively and the output is 5710.

BiPredicate<T,U>

This functional interface represents a predicate or Boolean valued function of two arguments. The type parameter of T represents the first argument to the predicate and U is the second argument to the predicate. Below is an example of the interface in action:

```
import java.util.function.BiPredicate;

public class FunctionTest {

    public static void main(String[] args) {

        BiPredicate<String, String> biPred = (x, y)
        -> x.length() > y.length();

        System.out.println(biPred.test("Doug",
        "Dougie"));

        System.out.println(biPred.negate().
        test("Doug", "Dougie"));

    }

}
```

There are two new methods which belong to the `BiPredicate` interface that you may not be familiar with. They are `test()` and `negate()`. The `test()` method does as its name indicates and tests the function, and the `negate()` method takes the negation of the result. The result that's printed when the code is run is `false` and `true`.

Interface UnaryOperator<T>

This interface denotes an operation on an operand which produces a result of the same type as the operand. Remember, operand is the element that's being manipulated in an expression and the operator is the symbol that's doing the manipulation. Below is an example of the interface in action:

```
import java.util.function.UnaryOperator;
```

```
public class FunctionTest {

    public static void main(String[] args) {

        UnaryOperator<Character> characters =
        UnaryOperator.identity();

        System.out.println(characters.apply('A'));

    }

}
```

Method reference

One new operator in Java 8 that we haven't discussed thus far is known as the method reference. The symbol that's used to represent this operator is two colons (::). This operator allows you to call an existing method by its name.

You can use forEach combined with the :: operator to iterate over a collection. An example of this is listed below:

```
import java.util.Arrays;

import java.util.List;


public class FunctionTest {

    public static void main(String[] args) {

        List<Integer> t = Arrays.asList(5, 10, 15,
        20, 25);

        t.forEach(System.out::println);

    }

}
```

The output is: 5, 10, 15, 20, 25

Chapter 9 Re-factored

This chapter has provided an overview of lambdas in Java. You learned about its benefits, how to create them, and how to use some of the premade functional interfaces in the Java API. Lambdas are a new functionality in Java that's going to be around for a long time, so it's a good investment to explore them further. Since lambdas introduce new syntax and a new way of way of programming in Java, it may take some time for everything to sink in. This is natural part of the learning process so keep coding with them and play around with the function package in the Java api.

Below is a brief recap about lambdas in Java:

- Lambdas are created from functional interfaces, previously known as single abstract methods (SAM) as these types of interfaces only have one abstract method.

- The basic lambda syntax is like a *reduced fat* version of a method. It has parameters followed by an arrow, and then the body details.

- You can drop the types of a lambda expression if the compiler knows enough to infer the type of the expression

- For simple lambda expressions you can remove the curly braces.

- A lambda with one parameter doesn't need any parenthesis. For example, the lambda expression of `(y) -> y + 1` can be rewritten like `y -> y + 1.`

Chapter 9 Resources

Java Function package: https://docs.oracle.com/javase/8/docs/api/java/util/function/package-summary.html

Chapter 9 Questions

1. T or F: A functional interface has exactly one abstract method.

2. T or F: Instances of functional interfaces can be created with lambda expressions and method references.

3. T or F: Functional interfaces can be annotated with `@Interface.`

4. T or F: Examples of functional interfaces in Java are `java.lang.Runnable,` `java.util.Comparator,` `java.lang.AutoCloseable,` and interfaces in the `java.util.function` package.

5. T or F: "SAM" is an acronym for single abstract modifier.

6. T or F: You can use a lambda expression to create the equivalent of an anonymous inner class from a normal interface.

7. T or F: A valid syntax for a lambda expression is as follows: (`parameter list`) `-> expression`

8. T or F: The types in a functional interface are optional.

9. T or F: A lambda expression can be thought of as an anonymous function.

10. T or F: The set of predefined functional interfaces are in the `java.util.function` package.

11. T or F: A lambda expression consists of two parts: One that's left of the arrow (`->`) which lists its parameters, and one that's right of the arrow which contains its body.

12. T or F: It's legal to supply a lambda expression anytime an object of an interface with a single abstract method is expected.

13. T or F: Lambdas can also be created using a new type called `function`.

14. T or F: It's legal to include a parameter or local variable in the lambda expression that has the same name as a local variable.

15. T or F: To create a new lambda expression in Java you must follow these steps. Create a functional interface and then in a separate class create the lambda expression using the functional interface as its type.

16. T or F: A functional interface can only have one lambda expression associated with it.

17. T or F: A lambda is similar to a method in that they both can't be passed around as arguments.

18. 18. T or F: If an interface declares an abstract method that overrides a public method of `java.lang.Object,` then that doesn't count towards the interface abstract method count.

19. T or F: The following expression is a valid one in Java.

    `TheTruth result = (int x) -> x == 0;`

20. An example of a functional interface that correctly uses the functional interface annotation is listed below:

    `public class Functional {`

    `@FunctionalInterface`

    `public interface FunctionalInterFaceDemo {`

```
    public void executeThisBaby();

  }

}
```

21. Look at the following lambda expression:

```
() -> System.out.println("Howdy!");
```

Create an associated functional interface and then complete the rest of the code so that it will compile.

22. What's a possible reason why functional interfaces can't have more than one abstract method?

Chapter 9 Answers

1. True. Even though functional interfaces can have multiple static and default methods, they can have precisely one abstract method.

2. True.

3. False. The annotation for it should be @FunctionalInterface

4. True. These are all examples of functional interfaces in the Java api.

5. False, it's an acronym for single abstract method.

6. False: You can only do this by using a functional interface.

7. True.

8. True. You may exclude them but including them in your code is legal albeit it makes your code more verbose.

9. True.

10. True.

11. True.

12. True.

13. False. There's no such type as function in Java.

14. False. This is not permissible.

15. True.

16. False. You can create 500 lambda expressions if you want as long as the parameters of the lambdas match that of the interface.

17. False. Lambdas can be passed around as arguments which are a feature that distinguishes it from a method.

18. True. Any implementation of the interface will also have an implementation of `java.lang.Object`.

19. True.

20. True.

21.

```
interface JustPrint {

    void print();

}


public class Test {

    public static void main(String[] args) {

        JustPrint someThing = () -> System.out.
        println("Howdy");

        someThing.print();

    }

}
```

22. The Java compiler infers the return type of a lambda expression by matching it's parameters with that of the associated interface. Having an interface with multiple abstract methods could confuse the compiler on which one to use if there are multiple methods that have identical signatures. Let's take a look at a traditional interface like the following:

```
interface Intro {

    void hello();

    void whatsGoingOn();

    void WhatsUp();

}
```

The following will compile without errors even though they all have identical method signatures. The reason for this is because any class that implements it must override the method by creating a body for it. Therefore, when an instance of a class is created and one of the overridden methods is called, there's no ambiguity about which method is being invoked. However, a lambda is not identical to a method and don't explicitly override the abstract method it's associated with. Therefore, functional interfaces work nicely with lambdas as having one abstract method that maps to a lambda reduces ambiguity.

Chapter 10: Java Classes

Congratulations on making it to the final chapter of this book! We're going to tour several classes in the Java API. This section was intentionally saved until the end. This allowed you to build your Java programming skills and also equipped you with the knowledge to make sense of the classes in the Java API. It's important for developers to be familiar with what the classes do so that they can reuse them in their programs to help speed up development. In the business world time is money, and being able to quickly introduce new quality software into the marketplace is of high importance. In this chapter we're going to learn which class is important when dealing with financial data, how to read in files from your computer, and an intro to JavaFX.

Mathematics

When I was in high school I was fortunate to have a TI-89 calculator which came with a myriad of mathematical operations. When I went to college students taking Calculus had to use software known as Maple. This opened up the possibilities of using computers to solve some of the biggest problems someone can face in a life-time...homework. Java has basic mathematical operations built into the core of its language via primitive types. However, there's a class located in the `java.lang` package that provides programmers additional mathematical functionality. Let's explore this class and learn how to turn Java into our very own dynamic calculator.

A Tour of the Math Class

The Math class has two fields and 73 methods. This class contains methods for basic exponential, logarithm, square root, and trigonometric functions. Let's take a look at one of the fields in the class which is the E field listed below:

`public static final double E`

This field uses `public`, `static`, and `final` modifiers. Remember, the `public` modifier means that the field can be used everywhere in the program, `static` means that this field is a class variable, and `final` means that the field cannot be changed. The type double denotes that it's an IEEE 754 double precision floating-point number.

To use just the Math class use the following code snippet: `import java.lang.Math;`

Or, you can mass import classes under the math package by using the following snippet: `import java.math.*;`

You can access the fields of the class by using `Math.E` or `Math.PI` as shown in the code snippets below:

`double eulersNumber = Math.E;`

`System.out.println(eulersNumber);`

The output is: `2.718281828459045`

Let's explore some trigonometric methods like sine, cosine, and tangent. The corresponding static methods for computing these values are `sin()`, `cos()`, and `tan()`. All of these methods accept a double as an argument.

`System.out.println(Math.sin(155.0));`

`System.out.println(Math.cos(.0156));`

`System.out.println(Math.tan(90.0));`

The output is listed below:

`-0.8733119827746476`

`0.9998783224676504`

`-1.995200412208242`

To convert an angle measured in radians to degrees you can use the `toDegrees()` method as shown below: `double a = Math.toDegrees(5.0);`

The output is: `286.4788975654116`

The `Math` class has several algebraic and arithmetic operations. To return the absolute value of a number use the `abs()` method which has five overrides for any integral primitive type. For example, the following snippet of code returns the absolute value of the following statement:

```
int absolute = Math.abs(-26272 + 1029);
```

The output is: `25243`

To take the square root of a double use the `sqrt()` method. For example, the following statement shows how to use the square root method:

```
double root = Math.sqrt(6.272);
```

The output when printed is: `2.5043961347997645`.

The `ceil()` and `floor()` methods accepts type `double` and rounds up or down to the nearest integer respectively.

The following code snippets showcases these methods in action:

```
double ceil = Math.ceil(5.3783);
```

```
double floor = Math.floor(9.37383);
```

The output is: `6.0` and `9.0`.

To round a number use the round() method. The following code snippet shows the method in action:

```
double round = Math.round(5.3363);
```

The output is: `5.0`

To calculate the hypotenuse or the longest side of a right triangle use the hypot() method. The following code snippet shows the method in action:

```
double longestSide = Math.hypot(5, 9);
```

```
10.295630140987
```

We can also raise one number to the power of another by using the `pow()` method. An example of this code in action is listed below:

```
double power = Math.pow(5,2);
```

The output is: 25.0

A Tour of BigDecimal

The `BigDecimal` class provides operations for arithmetic, scale manipulation, comparison, format conversion, and hashing. This class also allows programmers to specify scale or the number of digits after the mantissa (decimal point), and it provides the ability to state a rounding method. It's recommended to use this class when building applications that deals with money as currency typically require a specific type of precision such as two digits after the decimal place. To further understand the usefulness of `BigDecimal` when dealing with currencies let's look at code snippets that compare a `double` with `BigDecimal`.

```
double a = 0.07 - 0.05;
```

```
System.out.println(a);
```

Output is: `0.020000000000000004`

The above number wouldn't be helpful in a financial application. To avoid this from happening let's check out BigDecimal.

```
BigDecimal a = new BigDecimal(".07");
```

```
BigDecimal b = new BigDecimal(".05");
```

```
BigDecimal c = a.subtract(b);
```

```
System.out.println(c);
```

Output is: `0.02`

To use the `BigDecimal` class you must import it which is: `import  java.math.BigDecimal;`

Since BigDecimal is an object we must call one of its constructors. The syntax for doing so is listed below:

```
BigDecimal variableName = new BigDecimal("number");
```

This translated into Java code is listed below:

```
BigDecimal a = new BigDecimal("10.257");
```

As you can see we're actually passing a numeric String into the constructor. Let's look at the code if the quotes were removed.

```
BigDecimal a = new BigDecimal(10.257);
```

The output in this case when a is printed would be: `10.25699999999999967 315034155035391449928283691140625`

This is not exactly the kind of results we were hoping hence the use for the numeric

String in the constructor. When you pass a double to the constructor it's converting the actual value of a double into BigDecimal. The purpose of BigDecimal is to provide as much precision as possible and that's what's happening in this case.

To perform arithmetic operations on BigDecimals you can't use the binary operators like +, -, *, or / as these are not primitive values that we're manipulating. Instead, the BigDecimal class provides methods for manipulating the values of BigDecimal types like `add()`, `subtract()`, `divide()`, and `multiply()`.

Since BigDecimal is immutable you can only provide values through the use of a constructor. The below code creates an array of BigDecimals, multiples each element by 2, and then sets the scale of the results to include two decimal points using HALF_UP as the rounding mode.

Figure 10.0: BigDecimal demo.

```
BigDecimal[] a = new BigDecimal[5];

    a[0] = new BigDecimal(262);

    a[1] = new BigDecimal(7363);

    a[2] = new BigDecimal(362.3839);

    a[3] = new BigDecimal(383837.38393);

    a[4] = new BigDecimal(36732.83838);

    for (int i = 0; i < a.length; i++) {

        a[i] = a[i].multiply(new BigDecimal(2)).
        setScale(2, RoundingMode.HALF_UP);

        System.out.println(a[i]);

    }
```

The output is:

524.00

14726.00

724.77

767674.77

73465.68

Random

This is a class to use for generating pseudorandom numbers. It includes 2 constructors and 22 methods. Randomness has many applications and is used in statistics, probability, cryptography, gaming, and in games of chance (think Vegas). In order to create a new random number generator you must import its class and then invoke its constructor. To import its class use the following syntax:

```
import java.util.Random;
```

To create random objects use the following syntax:

```
Random obj = new Random();
```

To fetch the next random number you can use the `nextInt()` method. Let's create a random number generator that randomly prints 100 numbers within the range of 1-100. You can set the bound by passing the value into the `nextInt()` method. Here's one way to do this:

Figure 10.1: Random number generator.

```
import java.util.Random;


public class RandomTest {
public static void main(String[] args) {
    int i = 1;
    Random nums = new Random();
    do {
        int a = (nums.nextInt(100));
        System.out.println(a);
        i++;
    } while (i < 101);
  }
}
```

There will be 100 integers printed pseudo randomly within the range of 1-100.

The Scanner Class

This class hosts the methods for a simple text scanner that parse primitive types and Strings using regular expressions. In order to use this class we need to import it which can be done with the following snippet of code: `import java.util.Scanner;`

In order to use the scanner you must invoke one of its constructors like in the following snippet of code: `Scanner scan = new Scanner(System.in);`

`System.in` is an input stream which in this case connects the keyboard input to the console. This allows us to read in input from the keyboard to use in our programs. The `hasNext()` method has a return type of boolean and returns true if the scanner has another token in its input. Here's an example of the method in action:

```
boolean truth = scan.hasNext();

System.out.println(truth);
```

To force the output to be `false` you can terminate the program after it's ran. To do this on a windows operated machine use the keyboard combination of Ctrl + z, or Control-D on Mac OSX/Linux powered operating systems. This tells the stream that we have reached the End-of-file and that there's no more data to be read.

The `hasNext()` method has three overrides. The version that we'll investigate is the method with these details:

```
boolean hasNext(Pattern pattern)
```

As you can see from the above method details this method accepts a parameter of type Pattern. Therefore, we need to import the Pattern class and then invoke it. This can be done by the following snippet of code:

```
import java.util.regex.Pattern;

Pattern text = Pattern.compile(".");
```

Note, invoking type `Pattern` is a little different than what we're accustomed to. A regular expression which is denoted as a String must first be compiled in order to be used. The next step is to pass the Pattern reference variable into the `hasNext()` method as indicated below:

```
boolean match = scan.hasNext(text);
```

The dot (.) inside of the compile method means that it returns `true` for all characters—this includes alphanumeric and numeric characters. There are several predefined character classes which makes searching for certain character sequences simple. For example, \d allows you to search for any digit [0-9], and \w allows you to search for any word [a-zA-Z_0-9]. If you were to use \d in your code it would look like the following:

```
Pattern text = Pattern.compile("\\d");
```

The extra backslash is needed because excluding will lead to a compile error.

If you want to read in a String or primitive type then you'll need to use one of the flavors of the next() methods. As indicated below.

Figure 10.2: Table of Scanner class methods.

Type	Method
String	next()
byte	nextByte()
short	nextShort()
int	nextInt()
long	nextLong()
float	nextFloat()
double	nextDouble()
boolean	nextBoolean()

For example, the following code creates a Scanner object, an array of Strings with size 10, and then reads in user input into the array. It then converts each String to uppercase:

Figure 10.3: Converting text read in via the Scanner class.

```
Scanner read = new Scanner(System.in);

String[] text = new String[10];

for (int i = 0; i < 10; i++) {

    text[i] = read.next();

    text[i] = text[i].toUpperCase();

    }

    System.out.println("\n");
```

```
System.out.println("Converted output:");
for (String i : text) {
    System.out.println(i);
}
```

If you want to check if the next input in the scanner is a double you can use `hasNextDouble()`. If you want to read in input into the Scanner as a `double` you can use the `nextDouble()`. The following code shows how to read in doubles into the Scanner and then compute the total, count, and average of the numbers:

Figure 10.4: Calculating total, count, and average with Scanner.

```
import java.util.Scanner;


public class Average {
    public static void main(String[] args) {
        double sum = 0;
        double count = 0;
        Scanner scan = new Scanner(System.in);
        System.out.println("Enter in any double");
        System.out.println("The program will
        calculate: total and average");
        System.out.println("Press  any  character  to
        exit");
        while (scan.hasNextDouble()) {
            sum += scan.nextDouble();
            count++;
        }
        System.out.println("The total is " + sum);
        System.out.println("The  count  is  "  + (int)
        count);
        System.out.println("Average  is  "  +  sum  /
        count);

    }

}
```

How to read data from a file into the Scanner object

The Scanner class allows you to read in files so that you can manipulate it. However, before we can successfully read in files we need to learn about something called exception handling. So, we'll take a little detour and then come back to learning how to read in files.

Introduction to Exceptions

We learned how to construct arrays earlier in this book, and one of the common mistakes that beginners make is that they try to access an index in an array that doesn't exist. This type of error occurs during runtime and is known as an `Array-IndexOutOfBounds` error. That is an example of one of many exceptions in Java. For example, if you try and divide an integer by 0 then you'll get an `ArithmeticException` error, or if you create a null reference variable and try to use it to invoke a method then you'll get a `NullPointerException` error. Being able to anticipate potential errors in an app, and more importantly writing code to process it is an important skill that programmers should have under their belt. The approach to doing this in Java is by constructing `try-catch` blocks.

There are two keywords that you need to get familiar with in order to write try-catch blocks which are `try` and `catch`. An example of the syntax is shown below:

```
try {

    // statements

    } catch (Exception name) {

        // statements

    }
```

Let's look at an example.

Figure 10.5: Try catch block example.

```
int[] listOfStudnets = new int[10];

        try {

            for (int i = 0; i <= 10; i++) {

                listOfStudnets[i] = i * 2;

            }

        } catch (ArrayIndexOutOfBoundsException e) {
```

```
            System.err.println("Incorrect bounds
            for array");

    }
```

This code creates an array of size 10, and then does some computations on the elements of the array. However, there's one issue. The interval for the for loop is incorrectly set as it does 11 total iterations instead of 10. Therefore, when it tries to access the eleventh element it will cause an `ArrayIndexOutOfBoundsException` error to happen. However, this error was caught in the catch block and an error message was printed which provides hints on what the issue was.

You can also include a `finally` statement which will always execute once the try block exits. This section is typically reserved for cleaning up code that was over-looked by a `return, continue,` or `break` statement. In addition it's also a great place to prevent resource leaks. It's recommended by Oracle to close files within a finally block.

An example of a finally block is shown in the code snippet below. It uses the File class to read in a text file, read in their numbers, and then print them to the console. The finally block closes the Scanner. You need to use import `java.io.File` in order to get the program to work.

Figure 10.6: Reading in files using a Scanner.

```
Scanner scan = null;

    try {

            scan = new Scanner(new File("MyNumbers.
            txt"));

            while (scan.hasNextLong()) {

                    long nums = scan.nextLong();

                    System.out.println(nums);

            }

    } catch (Exception e) {

            System.err.println("File not found.Re-
            check your path.");

    } finally {

            if (scan != null) {
```

```
            scan.close();

    }

}

System.out.println(scan);
```

Intro to Java FX

JavaFX is the future of GUI for Java. Don't take my word for it; Oracle said themselves *that they plan to make JavaFX a replacement for Swing.* They also said that Swing will remain part of the Java SE in the foreseeable future. A reason for that is most likely the number of businesses that used Swing in the past. However, with Oracle officially stating that JavaFX is a replacement for Swing coupled with the strong number of Java developers it makes JavaFX worthwhile to learn.

JavaFX comes with a myriad of powerful features such as an extensive Java library, built in UI controls, 3D graphics features, and a high performance media engine to name a few. It also has been used in many real world projects in a variety of industries such as hospitals, dispatching, finance, trading, and aviation to name a few. Now that I'm done selling you on the benefits of JavaFX, let's learn how to first set it up on Eclipse.

Integrating JavaFX with an IDE

Coding applications with Java FX will start to become a pain if you don't have an IDE. There will be many different classes to work with, and importing them with the assistance of an IDE would be a tremendous time saver. There are a variety of IDEs out there in which you can develop Java programs with. The ones that I would recommend looking at are NetBeans, IntelliJ IDEA, and Eclipse. The one that you should use is totally up to you, but for the examples in this chapter I'll be using Eclipse.

Eclipse

There's a JavaFX plugin you can install for Eclipse called e(fx)clipse which comes with many features catered for building and deploying JavaFX applications. For those who are unfamiliar with Eclipse, it's a popular IDE that's well suited for building enterprise applications. If you're doing simple web development like HTML, CSS, and some javascript then using an IDE like Eclipse may be overkill. Eclipse IDEs all have version names like Kepler, Luna, Mars, Neon, and Oxygen. The versions that e(fx)clipse is compatible with is Mars(4.5), Neon(4.6), and Oxygen(4.7). Below are the steps on how to install e(fx)clipse with those versions of Eclipse.

Open up Eclipse. If you haven't downloaded it yet you can do so by visiting this url: `https://eclipse.org/downloads`

Make sure that the version you download is Mars, Neon, or Oxygen.

Install New Software: To install new software, click on the "Help" tab in Eclipse which is the menu tab located farthest to the right. Once that's done select install new software as indicated in the screenshot below:

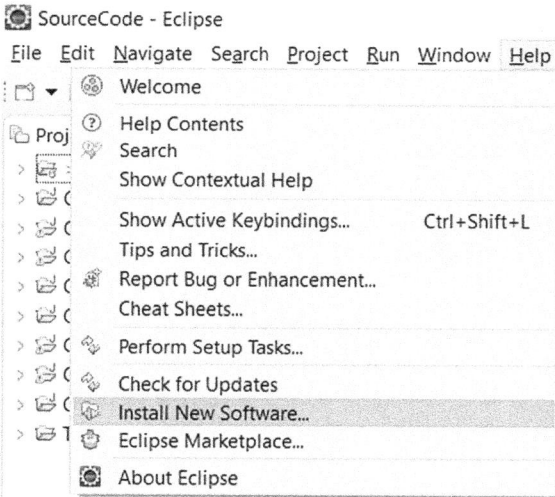

Enter the location of the e(fx)clipse plugin in the "Work with" field which is this url: `http://download.eclipse.org/efxclipse/updates-released/2.4.0/site`

Click the "Add" button, enter the name as e(fx)clipse or select any other name you desire. Enter the location as: `http://download.eclipse.org/efxclipse/updates-released/2.4.0/site` and then click the "OK" button.

Click install in order to install the e(fx)clipse IDE and then click the Next > button.

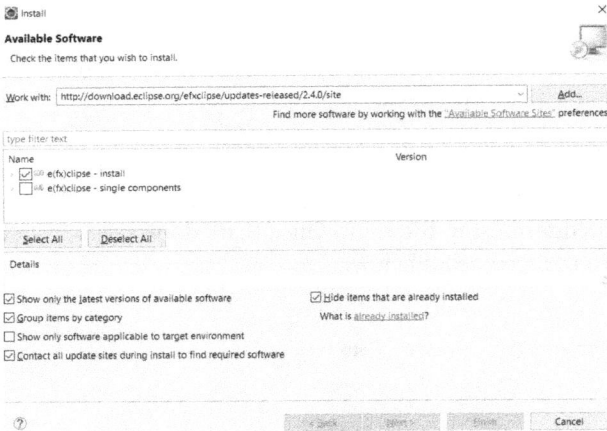

After you select Next >, you will be directed to another dialog box that'll allow you to review the items to be installed. Click the Next > button, and then select the terms of the license agreement. Once done click the "Finish" button and the plugin will began installation.

Once the installation is complete, a dialog box will open asking you if you would like to restart Eclipse. Click the "Yes" button in order for the changes take effect. Once that's done you're ready to start using JavaFX on Eclipse. The next step is to create a JavaFX project to ensure that everything is setup correctly.

To create a new JavaFX project click File -> New -> Project, and scroll down and select JavaFX as indicated in the screenshot below:

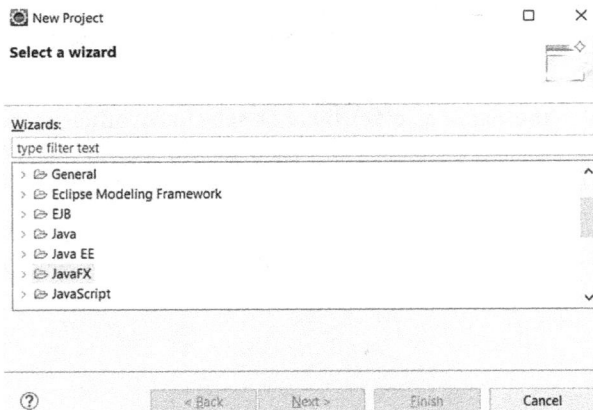

Once that's done, select Next > and then enter the project name like "HelloWorld" for example. A folder named "HelloWorld" should automatically be created, and inside the package application you'll see a file called `Main.java`—go ahead and open it. What you'll see is a default file with the following code:

Figure 10.7: Sample JavaFX demo.

```java
import javafx.application.Application;

import javafx.stage.Stage;

import javafx.scene.Scene;

import javafx.scene.layout.BorderPane;


public class Main extends Application {

    @Override

    public void start(Stage primaryStage) {

        try {

            BorderPane root = new BorderPane();

            Scene scene = new Scene(root, 400, 400);

            scene.getStylesheets().add(getClass().
            getResource("application.css").
            toExternalForm());

            primaryStage.setScene(scene);

            primaryStage.show();

        } catch (Exception e) {

            e.printStackTrace();

        }

    }


    public static void main(String[] args) {

        launch(args);

    }

}
```

As you can see, an IDE saves lots of time when coding. We're going to run the application to confirm that everything is setup properly. You can do this in Eclipse by selecting Run->Run in the menu items, or you can click the Run button which looks like the following icon .

The output should look like the following which is just an empty window:

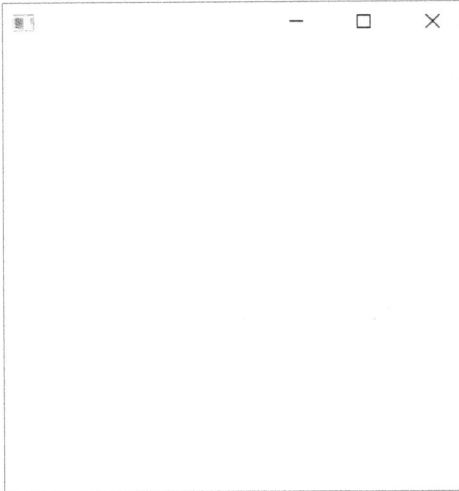

If everything ran successfully then congratulations, you have created and ran your first JavaFX program.

Even though an IDE helps us to create software quicker, we still need to still understand what's happening in the code in order to build something greater. Let's analyze `Main.java` line-by-line so that we get a better feel of JavaFX.

Main.java Blow-by-blow Analysis

Let's start at the very beginning of the file with a package statement followed by several import statements as shown below:

```
package application;

import javafx.application.Application;

import javafx.stage.Stage;

import javafx.scene.Scene;

import javafx.scene.layout.BorderPane;
```

What the statement `package   application` does is it creates a package named `application` in which `Main.java` goes in. This is considered a good oop practice as it helps keeps the program files organized as it groups related files together. Let's analyze the first of the four import statements:

```
import javafx.application.Application;
```

The first import statement includes the `Application` class which is the class in which JavaFX application extends. It's also considered the entry point for JavaFX applications.

```
import javafx.stage.Stage;
```

The Stage class is the top level JavaFX container for a JavaFX app.

```
import javafx.scene.Scene;
```

The Scene class is the container for all content in a scene graph. The default color for the scene is white, but that can be modified.

```
import javafx.scene.layout.BorderPane;
```

The `BorderPane` class contains details on how to manipulate the positioning of its children. `BorderPane` has a layout of: top, bottom, left, right, and center positions.

Now that we have a general understanding of the purpose of the four input classes, let's move on. Look at the following snippets of code:

```
public class Main extends Application { ... }
```

Main is the name of this demo class and as mentioned previously `Application` is the abstract class from which all JavaFX applications extend from and is considered the entry point for JavaFX applications. The class you create for your JavaFX application must extend Application or less a compile error will occur.

```
@Override

public void start(Stage primaryStage){ ... }
```

This is the main entry point for all JavaFX applications. This method is invoked after the `init()` method, or the method that initializes the application is returned. The `start()` method is listed in the Application class, and if you read its details you'll notice that it's an abstract method which means it's created with only a method signature and therefore the details of its body is left unimplemented. That means that we as the programmer must implement it. The `start()` method has a type parameter of `Stage primaryStage`, and represents the primary stage for which the scene can be set. The primary stage will be embedded into a browser if the application is launched as an applet. Next is the `try` block portion which is the most complicated portion of this demo but still straightforward. Let's analyze each statement.

```
try {... }
```

This represents the try block, and means that the program will try to execute the following statements.

```
BorderPane root = new BorderPane();
```

This constructs a `BorderPane` which will be used in the next statement.

```
Scene scene = new Scene(root,400,400);
```

This is one of the six scene constructors in the Scene class. This constructor has three parameters which are root, width, and height. The root was the BorderPane reference variable we created in the previous example, and the width and height are both set to 400 pixels.

```
scene.getStylesheets().add(getClass().
getResource("application.css").toExternalForm());
```

This is a series of five method calls. It starts with the **scene** reference variable which is used to invoke the **getStylesheets()** method which fetches a list of String URLS linking to the style sheets to use with the scene's content. The **add()** method belongs to `java.util.List` adds the following elements to a list. Inside the add() method is the getClass() method which returns the runtime class of the object. The getResource() method looks for a resource with the given name and in this case it's application.css. The last method creates a String representation of the url.

```
primaryStage.setScene(scene);
```

The details of the previous statement are sent as an argument to the setScene()method. As the name of the method suggests, it sets the scene to be used on the stage.

```
primaryStage.show();
```

As the name of the method suggests, the show is attempted to be seen by setting the visibility equal to true.

```
catch(Exception e) { e.printStackTrace(); }
```

This portion of the code will catch any errors such as `getResource("application.css")` being renamed to `getResource("")`.

```
public static void main(String[] args) { launch(args); }
```

Inside of the main method is a method called launch which purpose is to launch a standalone application.

Below is a recap of the lifecycle of a JavaFX application whenever an application is launched.

- Creates an instance of the Application class

- Calls the `init()` method

- Calls the `start()` method

- Wait for the application to terminate which happens when one of the following happens.

  - The app invokes Platform.exit

  - The last window has been closed

- The `stop()` method is called

Modifying Main.java

Now that we have we have a firm understanding of the basics for creating a JavaFX program, let's modify the existing demo program that we just created. Some of the things we're going to modify are the background color of the scene, and the width and height of the BorderPane. To modify the color of the background we need to modify this portion of the code:

```
Scene scene = new Scene(root,400,400);
```

We can modify the color of the scene by adding a color as the last argument. To add a color, use one of the constants from `javafx.scene.paint.Color`. We're going to add the color DARKGRAY. Also, we can modify the dimensions of the scene by changing the width and height. I want the scene to be twice as tall as it is wide, so let's set the width to 200 and keep the height to 400. The updated snippet of code is listed below:

```
Scene scene = new Scene(root,200,400,Color.DARKGRAY);
```

The output looks like the following:

In addition to using one of the constants, we can create our own mixture of color by using the Color constructor. You can use RGB, hexadecimal, or HSL to create your color codes. Every color has an implicit alpha value of 1.0 or an explicit one provided by the constructor. The alpha value represents the transparency of a color and can be within the ranges of 0.0-1.0, or 0-255. An alpha value of 1.0 or 255 means that the image is opaque, and an alpha value of 0 or 0.0 means that the color is transparent.

To create a color using rgb use the following syntax:

```
Color myColor = Color.rgb(value, value, value,
alphaValue);
```

The first three arguments can be integers within the range of 0-255, and the last argument is the alpha value which can be within the range of 0 to 1.0. The alpha value may be omitted, and in this case it will assumed to be 1.0.

For example the two statements are both valid:

```
Color myColor1 = Color.rgb(250, 250, 200);
```

```
Color myColor2 = Color.rgb(255, 255, 255, .1);
```

You can create a color using hexadecimal by using Color.web as indicated in the following snippet of code:

```
Color myColor = Color.web("#4d0000");
```

HSB stands for hue, saturation, and brightness. To create a color via this method use the following syntax:

```
Color myColor = Color.hsb(hue, saturation, brightness,
optional explicit alpha);
```

The below snippet shows it in action:

```
Color myColor = Color.hsb(200,.50,1.0);
```

Drawing shapes

JavaFX has features which enable the drawing of a variety of shapes such as lines, ovals, rectangles, and arcs. Below is the code for drawing these shapes:

Figure 10.8: Drawing shapes with JavaFX.

```
package application;
```

```java
import javafx.application.Application;

import javafx.scene.Group;

import javafx.scene.Scene;

import javafx.scene.canvas.Canvas;

import javafx.scene.canvas.GraphicsContext;

import javafx.scene.paint.Color;

import javafx.scene.shape.ArcType;

import javafx.stage.Stage;


public class Shapes extends Application {

    @Override

    public void start(Stage primaryStage) throws
    Exception {

        primaryStage.setTitle("Shapes");

        Group root = new Group();

        Canvas canvas = new Canvas(300, 300); //
        boundaries of the canvas

        GraphicsContext graphics = canvas.
        getGraphicsContext2D();

        draw(graphics);

        root.getChildren().add(canvas);

        primaryStage.setScene(new Scene(root));

        primaryStage.show();

    }


    private void draw(GraphicsContext graphics) {

        graphics.setFill(Color.GREY);

        graphics.setStroke(Color.BLACK);
```

```
        graphics.setLineWidth(2.55);

        graphics.strokeLine(20, 20, 50, 75); //
        creates a line

        graphics.fillOval(20, 80, 50, 50); // creates
        a gray filled oval

        graphics.strokeOval(80, 80, 50, 50); //
        creates an oval

        graphics.fillOval(140, 80, 50, 50); //
        creates a gray filled oval

        graphics.strokeOval(200, 80, 50, 50); //
        creates an oval

        graphics.fillRect(20, 150, 100, 25); // creates
        a gray filled rectangle

        graphics.strokeRect(150, 150, 100, 25); //
        creates a rectangle

        graphics.fillArc(10, 200, 100, 50, 45, 100,
        ArcType.ROUND);

        graphics.strokeArc(100, 200, 100, 50, 45,
        100, ArcType.ROUND);

        graphics.fillArc(200, 200, 100, 50, 45, 100,
        ArcType.ROUND);
    }


    public static void main(String[] args) {

        launch(args);

    }
}
```

The output is listed below:

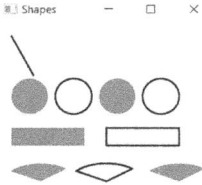

It looks difficult at first but after reading the explanation it will become easy to understand.

Blow-by-blow Analysis

In order to do this there are a couple of new things that we must learn in order to get started. Inside of the `start()` method we'll add a couple of new elements. We'll construct a `Group`, `Canvas`, `GraphicsContext`, and `draw()` method. A `Group` node creates an `ObservableList` of children that are rendered in order when the node is called. The Canvas is an image that can be drawn on. Think of it like the *digital version* of a canvas that artists draw on. The Canvas can be drawn on by using the `GraphicsContext` class, and the `draw()` method contains the instructions for drawing.

Inside of the `draw()` method there's a series of statements in which the reference variable to GraphicsContext is used to draw various shapes. There are a lot of new methods introduced which can be discovered by reading the class details of the appropriate shape. However, by observing the method names and tinkering with the code can provide you with some insights.

The `setFill()` method sets the color that the object will be filled with while the `setStroke()` method sets the current stroke of the paint attribute. The `setLineWidth()` method sets the width of the line, and the `strokeLine()` method creates the line. The `strokeLine()` method takes in four parameters which represent two points. The `fillOval()` and `strokeOval()` methods both create ovals. The difference between them is that `fillOval()` fills the oval with the current fill paint, and that `strokeOval()` creates an oval without no fill. The `fillRect()` and `strokeRect()` method both creates rectangles with the difference being that `fillRect()` fills up the rectangle while the other does not. The `fillArc()` and `strokeArc()` methods both creates arcs with the difference being that the `fillArc()` method fills the arc with color while the other does not. All of the instructions for drawing the shapes are placed in a method and then invoked in the `start()` method.

Creating buttons

JavaFX have features for creating buttons and other web elements. The code to create a button within a scene is shown below.

Figure 10.9: Creating buttons with JavaFX.

```java
package application;


import javafx.application.Application;

import javafx.scene.Scene;

import javafx.scene.control.Button;

import javafx.scene.layout.StackPane;

import javafx.stage.Stage;


public class Buttons extends Application {

    @Override

    public void start(Stage primaryStage) throws
    Exception {

        primaryStage.setTitle("Buttons");

        StackPane root = new StackPane();

        Button button = new Button();

        button.setText("Click Me");

        root.getChildren().add(button);

        Scene scene = new Scene(root, 200, 100);

        primaryStage.setScene(scene);

        primaryStage.show();

    }


    public static void main(String[] args) {
```

```
            launch(args);

    }

}
```

This code creates a simple button as indicated in the image below:

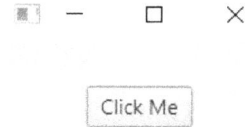

As you may have noticed, there are some elements from the previous example in this code. For example, the class extends the Application and there's both a start method and main method. There are a couple of new elements like `Button`, `StackPane`, and `setText()`. The Button constructor creates the button. The StackPane constructor is a container object and allows you to layout nodes, and the setText() method allows you to set the text of an object. However, a button alone is not very useful as it needs to be triggered to do some type of action. In order to make the button respond to an event when it's clicked you'll need to add an event listener to the Button object. Let's add this code right after this statement:

```
button.setText("Click Me");
```

The code to add will be something like this below:

```
public void start(Stage primaryStage) throws Exception {

        button.setOnAction(value -> {

            button.setText("Hey You!");

        });
```

What this does is it causes the button to change text once it's clicked.

Chapter 10 Re-factored

This is the final chapter of this book and it provided an overview of some of the classes in the Java API. However, there are over 4000 classes in Java SE 8, so explaining all of them are beyond the scope of this book. However, I would suggest studying the API and to constantly tinker with the different classes in the Java API. In the beginning of the book I was against the use of an IDE like Eclipse, but when you start working with multiple of classes and build bigger programs gaining familiarity with an IDE is essential. Not only does an IDE provide features for speeding up programming like auto completion and debugging, but they also suggest methods to use. To become a better Java programmer play with various classes and study how they're built. This will help provide insights to how to build oop programs in Java.

Chapter 10 Resources

IntelliJ IDEA: https://www.jetbrains.com/idea/download

Netbeans IDE version for Java SE: https://netbeans.org/downloads

Eclipse downloads: https://eclipse.org/downloads

Chapter 10 Questions

1.   T or F: The `java.lang.Object` class is considered the master class in Java, and all other classes inherit from it.

2.   T or F: The `BigDecimal` class should be used if you're building a financial application.

3.   T or F: The `Scanner` class only provides methods from reading in text from a console. It doesn't provide any methods to read in data from a file like a .txt one for example.

4.   T or F: A try block must have an associated catch block.

5.   T or F: A catch block can handle only one type of exception.

6.   T or F: A JavaFX app needs only a main method to run.

7.   T or F: A JavaFX class must extend a class known as Main.

Chapter 10 Answers

8.   True. This is the class in which every Java program extends.

9.   True. The `BigDecimal` class allows you to work around Java's arithmetic limitations.

10.   False. The Scanner class does provide the capability to read in data from a file.

11. False. It could have just the `try` and `finally` block.

12. False. As of Java SE 7 and later it can handle more than one type of exception.

13. False. It also needs a `start()` method.

14. False. It must extend a class known as `Application` and include an import for it.

Index

A

abstract class 172, 173, 174, 175, 176, 177, 178, 191, 195, 241, 286

access modifiers 25, 28, 113, 114, 131, 136, 138, 175, 181

accessor 128, 185

Addition 45, 257, 258

AND 49, 50, 51, 52, 53, 83

anonymous classes 185, 187, 188, 189

anonymous inner class 256, 265

arguments 118, 119, 122, 126, 138, 141, 143, 153, 155, 187, 222, 224, 236, 243, 245, 262, 263, 266, 268, 289

array class 225, 226

ArrayIndexOutOfBoundsException 219, 231, 280

ArrayList 231, 233, 234, 235, 236, 237, 238, 239, 240, 241, 242, 244, 253, 254

arrow token 258

Assignment 47

Associativity 53

autoboxing 242

B

behaviors 109, 160, 161, 163, 169, 170, 172, 176, 256

Behaviors 109

BigDecimal 272, 273, 274, 295

Big-O notation 240

Bit Shifts 51

Bitwise Complement 45

Bitwise Operators 51

boolean expression 65, 66, 67, 75, 76, 83, 96

booleans 36, 41, 96, 207

break statement 73, 81, 82, 280

byte 19, 20, 26, 30, 31, 32, 33, 36, 39, 40, 41, 45, 54, 55, 56, 58, 72, 123, 125, 138, 142, 219, 241, 277

C

caching 204

char 34, 36, 42, 54, 55, 56, 58, 72, 105, 106, 123, 125, 138, 142, 206, 207, 209, 211, 212, 227, 241

class diagrams 189, 191, 198, 200

Classes 108, 109, 111, 113, 115, 117, 119, 121, 123, 125, 127, 129, 131, 133, 135, 137, 139, 141, 143, 145, 151, 183, 184, 186, 201, 229, 241, 270, 271, 273, 275, 277, 279, 281, 283, 285, 287, 289, 291, 293, 295

class variable 110, 130, 271

code block 258

Collections 74, 159, 232, 233, 235, 236, 237, 238, 239, 241, 243, 245, 246, 247, 249, 251, 252, 253

command prompt 21, 22, 23, 25, 28, 29, 112, 224

compile 21, 25, 26, 27, 28, 29, 31, 34, 57, 66, 68, 80, 85, 88, 96, 97, 111, 112, 119, 126, 131, 143, 145, 147, 151, 152, 155,

158, 162, 173, 174, 175, 178, 181, 188, 194, 202, 206, 219, 223, 224, 231, 242, 246, 247, 252, 258, 260, 267, 269, 276, 277, 286

compile error 34, 66, 80, 85, 97, 111, 119, 131, 143, 145, 147, 151, 152, 155, 158, 162, 173, 174, 175, 178, 188, 194, 202, 223, 224, 246, 252, 277, 286

Compiler errors 26

complexity 130

concrete classes 174, 233, 234

Conditional Operator 51

constant 58, 111, 131, 162, 177, 241, 245, 250, 251

Constants 161, 162

continue statement 82, 102

control flow 65, 71, 73, 75, 76, 81, 82, 96, 97

C-programming language 110, 115

CPU 20

creating buttons 293

curly braces 24, 27, 65, 66, 68, 77, 83, 95, 96, 97, 115, 188, 258, 259, 265

D

data encapsulation 136

data structure 219, 240, 243, 246, 247, 248

diamond bracket 236

Division 46

dot operator 118, 123, 138, 142

double 32, 35, 36, 41, 42, 48, 54, 55, 56, 57, 58, 62, 64, 65, 96, 106, 111, 119, 123, 125, 138, 142, 162, 168, 193, 195, 198, 203, 206, 207, 208, 209, 214, 220, 222, 227, 231, 241, 271, 272, 273, 274, 277, 278

double precision floating-point number 271

doubly linked list 250

Doug Purcell iii, 17

Do while loop 75

dynamic memory management 115

E

Eclipse 29, 151, 281, 282, 283, 285, 294, 295

e(fx)clipse plugin 282

elements 27, 132, 169, 187, 217, 218, 219, 221, 222, 223, 224, 225, 230, 231, 234, 237, 238, 239, 240, 245, 247, 248, 249, 250, 251, 253, 254, 260, 280, 287, 292, 293, 294

Encapsulation 130, 182, 201

enhanced for loop 74, 221, 240, 251

enum 58, 97, 131, 132, 136, 139, 260

Equal 47

escape characters 208

exception handling 279

Expressions 64

F

Feels Good 24

fields 109, 113, 118, 120, 129, 130, 131, 137, 143, 146, 147, 149, 150, 162, 169, 170, 172, 173, 174, 182, 185, 187, 270, 271

Fields 109

First in First out 249

float 35, 36, 41, 43, 46, 47, 54, 55, 56, 58, 62, 123, 125, 138, 142, 229, 241, 277

functional programming 255, 257

function package 260, 261, 265, 266

G

garbage collection 110

generics 253

Greater than 48, 49

H

hashtable 250

hexadecimal 40, 41, 289

I

identifiers 57, 58, 110

IEEE 754 35, 55, 271

If-then-else statement 67, 68

If-then statement 66

Importing classes 112

inheritance 146, 147, 148, 158, 163, 195, 200, 202

inner loop 79, 80, 81

Instanceof 49

instance variables 109, 110, 119, 120, 121, 122, 123, 126, 127, 128, 130, 131, 137, 141, 143, 175, 182, 184

int 32, 33, 34, 36, 40, 41, 43, 44, 45, 46, 47, 51, 52, 54, 55, 56, 57, 58, 61, 62, 63, 64, 65, 70, 72, 73, 75, 80, 83, 84, 85, 86, 88, 89, 90, 97, 99, 102, 103, 104, 105, 106, 107, 109, 111, 113, 114, 116, 117, 118, 119, 122, 123, 125, 138, 150, 157, 158, 175, 187, 191, 193, 195, 198, 206, 209, 210, 211, 212, 213, 214, 217, 218, 220, 221, 223, 224, 225, 226, 227, 228, 230, 231, 235, 238, 241, 242, 243, 245, 252, 258, 260, 262, 266, 272, 277

integrated development environment 24

interface 19, 28, 58, 97, 112, 160, 161, 162, 163, 164, 165, 166, 167, 168, 169, 170, 174, 175, 176, 187, 191, 193, 194, 195, 198, 201, 232, 233, 234, 235, 236, 238, 239, 243, 245, 246, 249, 250, 251, 252, 254, 256, 257, 258, 259, 260, 261, 262, 263,

265, 266, 267, 268

Interfaces 146, 147, 149, 151, 153, 155, 157, 159, 160, 161, 162, 163, 165, 167, 169, 171, 173, 175, 176, 177, 179, 181, 183, 185, 187, 189, 191, 193, 195, 197, 199, 201

iterating over a Collection 238, 239, 240, 245

Iterator 239

J

Java API 108, 160, 161, 162, 203, 205, 235, 237, 256, 265, 270, 294

Java APIs 19

javac 21, 22, 23, 25, 26, 28, 29, 31, 112, 152, 247

java file 19, 25, 28, 29, 30, 112, 138, 139

JavaFX 270, 281, 283, 284, 285, 286, 288, 289, 293, 295

Java HotSpot 21, 23

Java Virtual Machine 19, 20, 30

JDK 20, 21, 26, 28, 29, 30, 31, 204

JRE 20, 21, 26, 29, 30, 31

Just in Time Compiler 20, 30

L

lambdas 255, 257, 258, 259, 260, 262, 264, 265, 268, 269

Left shift 52

legacy classes 246

Less than 48

lexicographical 250

LIFO 246, 247, 248

LinkedList 233, 234, 243, 244, 245

Literals 41

local classes 185, 186

local variable 28, 31, 77, 80, 117, 141, 222, 266

local variables 109, 110, 123, 141, 142, 186, 246

long 21, 32, 34, 36, 54, 55, 56, 57, 58, 64, 76, 110, 119, 123, 125, 142, 219, 228, 241, 255, 262, 265, 268, 277

loop 40, 74, 75, 76, 77, 78, 79, 80, 81, 82, 83, 88, 89, 90, 91, 92, 93, 94, 95, 96, 101, 102, 132, 220, 221, 238, 239, 240, 251, 280

M

main method 24, 25, 110, 118, 139, 164, 165, 170, 174, 187, 222, 223, 224, 243, 287, 294, 295

maintainability 136

Map 251, 252

Map interface 251, 252

marker interface 162

members 108, 113, 142, 144, 147, 152, 181, 182, 183, 184, 185, 186, 191, 229

method 24, 25, 62, 109, 110, 112, 113, 115, 116, 117, 118, 119, 127, 128, 130, 131, 132, 136, 137, 138, 139, 141, 142, 143, 147, 150, 151, 152, 157, 160, 161, 163, 164, 165, 166, 167, 170, 172, 173, 174, 175, 177, 179, 185, 187, 189, 191, 193, 196, 201, 204, 205, 206, 207, 209, 210, 211, 212, 213, 214, 216, 220, 221, 222, 223, 224, 225, 227, 228, 229, 231, 237, 238, 240, 242, 243, 244, 245, 246, 247, 248, 249, 250, 252, 255, 256, 257, 258, 261, 262, 263, 264, 265, 266, 267, 268, 269, 271, 272, 273, 275, 276, 279, 286, 287, 288, 289, 292, 294, 295, 296

method call 112, 117, 118, 119, 143

Method overriding 150

method signature 118, 258, 286

Modulus 46

multidimensional arrays 225

Multiplication 46

mutator 127

N

Narrowing primitive Conversions 56

nested classes 181, 182, 183, 202

nested loops 78, 225

non-argument constructor 122

non-static method 117

Not equal to 47

NullPointerException 279

O

object 24, 30, 49, 62, 71, 108, 109, 110, 114, 115, 117, 118, 121, 122, 123, 130, 131, 136, 137, 138, 141, 142, 143, 146, 150, 155, 159, 160, 162, 163, 167, 173, 174, 182, 183, 184, 185, 188, 189, 190, 200, 204, 205, 209, 210, 211, 214, 216, 217, 218, 223, 229, 230, 231, 241, 244, 245, 246, 250, 251, 252, 256, 266, 273, 277, 279, 287, 292, 294

object oriented programming 24, 108, 114, 136

octal 39, 40, 41

Octals 39

operand 42, 43, 48, 49, 52, 56, 263

OR 50, 51, 52, 53

outer loop 79, 80, 81

P

package-private 113, 150, 161, 172, 175, 181, 182, 191
packages 57, 111, 112, 113, 136, 139, 151

pairing keys to values 251

parameters 115, 116, 117, 118, 119, 121, 122, 126, 127, 138, 141,

143, 153, 176, 187, 222, 236, 247, 258, 259, 260, 265, 266, 268, 287, 292

PATH 29

polymorphism 146, 155, 159, 200

post decrement 44

post increment 44

Precedence 53

primitive types 32, 33, 35, 37, 39, 41, 43, 45, 47, 49, 51, 53, 55, 57, 59, 61, 63, 64, 66, 72, 114, 115, 142, 216, 229, 241, 270, 276

R

raw types 247

reference variable 114, 118, 165, 183, 185, 239, 246, 276, 279, 287, 292

regular expression 212, 276

reserved keywords in Java 57, 58

reserved keywords in Java 8 57, 58

return keyword 260

Right shift 52

Runtime errors 28

runtime memory management 248

S

Scanner Class 276

Semantic errors 27

semicolon 64, 96, 161, 188

short 17, 32, 33, 34, 36, 41, 50, 52, 54, 55, 56, 58, 72, 97, 123, 125, 142, 189, 208, 211, 241, 246, 277

signature 118, 126, 147, 150, 151, 256, 257, 258, 286

square brackets 220, 230, 231

Stack 233, 234, 245, 246, 247, 248, 253

statements 36, 64, 65, 66, 67, 71, 72, 73, 74, 75, 76, 77, 78, 81, 82, 83, 84, 86, 88, 96, 97, 115, 116, 117, 131, 133, 138, 139, 142, 143, 144, 150, 153, 155, 157, 185, 187, 188, 221, 230, 240, 259, 285, 286, 287, 289, 292

static 24, 25, 58, 109, 110, 111, 112, 117, 130, 131, 142, 162, 165, 167, 172, 174, 175, 181, 182, 183, 184, 185, 207, 211, 224, 227, 229, 234, 242, 254, 256, 267, 271, 287

static fields 131, 172, 174

Strings 71, 88, 203, 205, 206, 207, 209, 210, 211, 212, 213, 214, 215, 216, 221, 224, 248, 255, 276, 277

subclass 146, 147, 148, 149, 150, 151, 152, 157, 158, 163, 169, 178, 202, 234, 251

subscript notation 218

Subtraction 46

Super classes 147

Syntax errors 27, 31

System.out.println() 62, 68, 92, 103, 104, 105, 106, 112, 160, 203

System Variables 22, 28

T

Ternary 51

text editor 24

thread 250, 256, 257

U

Unicode 34, 36, 57, 60, 92, 94

use case 190, 191, 193, 196

V

variables 23, 55, 57, 64, 65, 77, 108, 109, 110, 111, 114, 116, 119, 120, 121, 122, 123, 126, 127, 128, 130, 131, 137, 141, 142, 143, 144, 151, 161, 174, 175, 182, 184, 186, 204, 246

void 24, 25, 58, 109, 115, 116, 117, 119, 120, 136, 138, 142, 143, 152, 161, 175, 191, 195, 198, 224, 260, 261, 267, 286, 287

W

Widening primitive Conversions 54